OPPOSING
VIEWPOINTS®
SERIES

Syria

Other Books of Related Interest

Opposing Viewpoints Series

Afghanistan

Egypt

The Palestinian Territories

US Foreign Policy

At Issue Series

Biological and Chemical Weapons

Does the World Hate the US?

Drones

Is Foreign Aid Necessary?

Current Controversies Series

Immigration

Pakistan

Politics and Religion

Racial Profiling

"Congress shall make no law . . . abridging the freedom of speech, or of the press."

First Amendment to the US Constitution

The basic foundation of our democracy is the First Amendment guarantee of freedom of expression. The Opposing Viewpoints Series is dedicated to the concept of this basic freedom and the idea that it is more important to practice it than to enshrine it.

OPPOSING VIEWPOINTS® SERIES

Syria

Noah Berlatsky, Book Editor

GREENHAVEN PRESS
A part of Gale, Cengage Learning

Farmington Hills, Mich • San Francisco • New York • Waterville, Maine
Meriden, Conn • Mason, Ohio • Chicago

Elizabeth Des Chenes, *Director, Content Strategy*
Douglas Dentino, *Manager, New Product*

For more information, contact:
Greenhaven Press
27500 Drake Rd.
Farmington Hills, MI 48331-3535
Or you can visit our Internet site at gale.cengage.com

For product information and technology assistance, contact us at

Gale Customer Support, 1-800-877-4253
For permission to use material from this text or product, submit all requests online at www.cengage.com/permissions

Further permissions questions can be emailed to permissionrequest@cengage.com

Articles in Greenhaven Press anthologies are often edited for length to meet page requirements. In addition, original titles of these works are changed to clearly present the main thesis and to explicitly indicate the author's opinion. Every effort is made to ensure that Greenhaven Press accurately reflects the original intent of the authors. Every effort has been made to trace the owners of copyrighted material.

Cover image copyright © vyskoczilova/Shutterstock.com.

LIBRARY OF CONGRESS CATALOGING-IN-PUBLICATION DATA

Syria / Noah Berlatsky, book editor.
    pages cm. -- (Opposing viewpoints)
    Includes bibliographical references and index.
    ISBN 978-0-7377-7006-3 (hardcover) -- ISBN 978-0-7377-7007-0 (paperback)
    1. Syria--Politics and government--2000- 2. Syria--Foreign relations--1971- 3. Syria--Foreign relations--United States. 4. United States--Foreign relations--Syria. I. Berlatsky, Noah, editor of compilation.
    DS98.6.S93 2014
    320.95691'0905--dc23
                                                    2014010807

Printed in the United States of America
1 2 3 4 5 6 7 18 17 16 15 14

Contents

Chapter 3: What Is the Status of the Syrian Refugee Crisis?

Chapter 4: What Is the Relationship Between Syria and the World?

Why Consider Opposing Viewpoints?

> "The only way in which a human being can make some approach to knowing the whole of a subject is by hearing what can be said about it by persons of every variety of opinion and studying all modes in which it can be looked at by every character of mind. No wise man ever acquired his wisdom in any mode but this."
>
> *John Stuart Mill*

In our media-intensive culture it is not difficult to find differing opinions. Thousands of newspapers and magazines and dozens of radio and television talk shows resound with differing points of view. The difficulty lies in deciding which opinion to agree with and which "experts" seem the most credible. The more inundated we become with differing opinions and claims, the more essential it is to hone critical reading and thinking skills to evaluate these ideas. Opposing Viewpoints books address this problem directly by presenting stimulating debates that can be used to enhance and teach these skills. The varied opinions contained in each book examine many different aspects of a single issue. While examining these conveniently edited opposing views, readers can develop critical thinking skills such as the ability to compare and contrast authors' credibility, facts, argumentation styles, use of persuasive techniques, and other stylistic tools. In short, the Opposing Viewpoints Series is an ideal way to attain the higher-level thinking and reading skills so essential in a culture of diverse and contradictory opinions.-

In addition to providing a tool for critical thinking, Opposing Viewpoints books challenge readers to question their own strongly held opinions and assumptions. Most people form their opinions on the basis of upbringing, peer pressure, and personal, cultural, or professional bias. By reading carefully balanced opposing views, readers must directly confront new ideas as well as the opinions of those with whom they disagree. This is not to argue simplistically that everyone who reads opposing views will—or should—change his or her opinion. Instead, the series enhances readers' understanding of their own views by encouraging confrontation with opposing ideas. Careful examination of others' views can lead to the readers' understanding of the logical inconsistencies in their own opinions, perspective on why they hold an opinion, and the consideration of the possibility that their opinion requires further evaluation.

Evaluating Other Opinions

To ensure that this type of examination occurs, Opposing Viewpoints books present all types of opinions. Prominent spokespeople on different sides of each issue as well as well-known professionals from many disciplines challenge the reader. An additional goal of the series is to provide a forum for other, less known, or even unpopular viewpoints. The opinion of an ordinary person who has had to make the decision to cut off life support from a terminally ill relative, for example, may be just as valuable and provide just as much insight as a medical ethicist's professional opinion. The editors have two additional purposes in including these less known views. One, the editors encourage readers to respect others' opinions—even when not enhanced by professional credibility. It is only by reading or listening to and objectively evaluating others' ideas that one can determine whether they are worthy of consideration. Two, the inclusion of such viewpoints encourages the important critical thinking skill of objectively evaluating an author's credentials and bias. This evaluation will illuminate an author's reasons for taking a particular stance on an issue and will aid in readers' evaluation of the author's ideas.

It is our hope that these books will give readers a deeper understanding of the issues debated and an appreciation of the complexity of even seemingly simple issues when good and honest people disagree. This awareness is particularly important in a democratic society such as ours in which people enter into public debate to determine the common good. Those with whom one disagrees should not be regarded as enemies but rather as people whose views deserve careful examination and may shed light on one's own.

Thomas Jefferson once said that "difference of opinion leads to inquiry, and inquiry to truth." Jefferson, a broadly educated man, argued that "if a nation expects to be ignorant and free . . . it expects what never was and never will be." As individuals and as a nation, it is imperative that we consider the opinions of others and examine them with skill and discernment. The Opposing Viewpoints Series is intended to help readers achieve this goal.

David L. Bender and Bruno Leone,
Founders

Introduction

> *"I was 16 and I was just like hearing every day those horror stories when people were coming [from the Hama massacre]. . . . I can start telling you books of stories from every person and what they saw over there."*
>
> *"Even now, all I can see from life is a black cloud following me and that has been with me for a long time."*
>
> Rana al-Hamwi,
> the pseudonym for an American
> schoolteacher whose relatives escaped
> from the 1982 massacre in
> the Syrian town of Hama by
> government troops attempting to quell
> an uprising by insurgents.

The ongoing Syrian civil war began in 2011, but its roots go back much further in Syrian history. The secular, nationalist Ba'ath Party of Syria has since the 1940s been opposed by the Muslim Brotherhood, a conservative religious group. The tension between the two was compounded by the fact that the Ba'ath Party was led by Alawites, a Muslim denomination considered heretical by the Muslim Brotherhood. The conflict between the Ba'ath and Muslim Brotherhood has often erupted in violence in Syria. Before the 2011 civil war, the worst clash had occurred in 1982 in the city of Hama.

The Ba'ath defense minister, Hafez al-Assad (father of the current Syrian president, Bashar al-Assad), became president of Syria in 1971. In 1976, Assad (also spelled *Asad*) intervened in the Lebanese civil war. In doing so, he inadvertently destabilized Syria itself. Secular and liberal protesters demanded democratic reforms. At the same time, the Muslim Brotherhood and related groups began what Robert Seale in *Asad, the Struggle for the Middle East*, called "a long campaign of terror" against the Ba'ath authorities, including bombings and assassination attempts. Assad responded with even more violence and repression. Mere membership in the Muslim Brotherhood was made a capital offense in 1980. But still the conflict dragged on.

Hama, in west-central Syria, was a hotbed of pro–Muslim Brotherhood sentiment. In February 1982 a government army unit searching the city was ambushed, sparking a general uprising in which some seventy police and government officials were killed. Islamists claimed control of the city and urged the rest of Syria to rise up as well.

Assad ordered an invasion of the city, warning that anyone who stayed in Hama would be considered a rebel. The siege of Hama lasted three weeks. It included air strikes and intense shelling. In a February 24, 1982, editorial, the British newspaper *The Guardian* reported on "merciless carnage carried out by the Government's private Alawite forces." The exact events are still uncertain, but there were accounts of widespread torture and possible use of poison gas.

David Arnold in a February 3, 2012, article for *Middle East Voices*, interviewed a Syrian woman who now teaches school in the United States, whose family members witnessed the violence. She described some of the numerous horrors in Hama, including an incident in which soldiers poured gasoline on a woman and her adult son and set them on fire, and another in which soldiers shot a fourteen-month-old baby. She added,

> Another member of my family, she refused to leave her home. She said nobody will come so I will stay inside the house. They came and they looted the house. She [had]

many gold bracelets on her wrists, so they cut off both of her hands and let her bleed to [death].

Rifaat Assad, the president's brother, is reported to have pumped diesel fuel into the tunnels under the city, which was then ignited, in order to smoke out rebels. He placed tanks at tunnel entrances to shell people as they tried to escape.

The death toll of the Hama massacre is still disputed. Thomas Friedman, in *From Beirut to Jerusalem*, reports that Rifaat claimed to have killed thirty-eight thousand people. Arnold, in the above-mentioned *Middle East Voices* article, estimates deaths at between ten thousand and forty-five thousand. The majority of those deaths would have been nonrebel civilians.

The assault on Hama is thought to be the worst massacre committed by an Arab leader against his own people in modern times. It has had long-term effects in Syria. Anne Alexander in a March 29, 2011, commentary for the BBC, argues that the violence in Hama effectively stifled opposition, so that "it was nearly 20 years before widespread dissent became public again."

When resistance did resurface, however, Hama was once again a focal point. Since 2011 and the beginning of the civil war, Hama has been a center of protest. Opposition forces held the city for six weeks in 2011 until a government assault in August recaptured it; at least a hundred civilians were killed. On the thirtieth anniversary of the original massacre, activists in Hama splashed red paint across the city, only to have government firetrucks wash it away, according to Azmat Khan in a February 2, 2012, article on the Public Broadcasting Service website. The legacy of the Hama massacre is harder to erase. There is little doubt that the violence Hafez Assad unleashed in the city continues to fuel the bitter resistance to his son Bashar.

The viewpoints in this book examine controversies regarding Syria under the following chapter headings: "What Should the US Role Be in Syria?," "What Is the Status of the Syrian Resistance?," "What Is the Status of the Syrian Refugee Crisis?," and "What Is the Relationship Between Syria and the World?" Each chapter includes different viewpoints on the important issues facing Syria and the international community as it struggles with civil war and the legacy of violence and repression epitomized by the massacre at Hama.

OPPOSING
VIEWPOINTS®
SERIES

CHAPTER 1

What Should the US Role Be in Syria?

Chapter Preface

In August and September of 2013, the United States faced a diplomatic crisis in Syria. President Bashar al-Assad appeared to have used chemical weapons against rebel forces in the nation's civil war, killing more than one thousand civilians. US president Barack Obama, who had declared that the United States would not tolerate the use of chemical weapons, called for air strikes on Syria, but was met with international and domestic political opposition. America seemed trapped, unable to either respond to the chemical attacks or to ignore them.

And then US secretary of state John Kerry made an off-hand remark suggesting that the situation could be defused if Assad agreed to give up all his chemical weapons. Russian president Vladimir Putin leapt on the comment, saying that Russia would facilitate the elimination of Syria's chemical weapons. Assad agreed. The United States agreed. The crisis was averted, at least for a while.

This diplomatic resolution has divided politcal pundits. Some have argued that allowing Russia to lead the way in Syria is a failure for the administration, and that the plan to rid Syria of chemical weapons is not feasible. In an October 4, 2013, article at *Business Insider*, for example, Michael Kelley argues that "the deal to disarm the Syrian regime's chemical weapons gives Bashar al-Assad and his allies a boost while clipping American influence in the region." Natasha Lennard in a September 10, 2013, piece on *Salon* said that "the chemical weapons handover initiative made Russia look a dove to America's hawkish leadership," and suggests that Obama was scrambling to take credit for Putin's idea.

But while some have seen the president as ineffective, others have argued that Obama and his team have achieved an impressive diplomatic coup. In a September 16, 2013, post on

Mother Jones magazine, Kevin Drum points out that the Obama administration managed to take a strong stand against chemical weapons and enlist Russian aid in disarming Syria without any military action. "Was this all just a lucky accident?" he wonders, and speculates that the administration may have coordinated with Russia and deliberately allowed Putin to take the credit. David Horsey in a November 19, 2013, article at the *Los Angeles Times* doubts that Obama's strategy was quite so planned out but still applauds the outcome. "Obama's foreign policy looks rather improvisational," he argues, "but that may not be quite as bad as the conservatives say it is. Improvisation in the name of peace is no vice."

This chapter looks at other controversies around the US approach to Syria policy. Different authors take opposing perspectives on issues such as direct military intervention in Syria, aid to Syrian rebels, and congressional approval of presidential military action.

> "I have decided that the United States should take military action against Syrian regime targets."

The United States Should Use Air Strikes Against Syria

Barack Obama

Barack Obama is the forty-fourth president of the United States. In the following viewpoint, he argues that the regime of Syrian president Bashar al-Assad has used chemical weapons against civilians, including children. He says that America must respond in order to protect the international order, which has declared chemical weapons to be illegal. The best response, he suggests, is not full-scale military intervention, but targeted bombing. He adds that he will seek support from Congress to make air strikes, though he believes he has the authority to order action without Congressional approval.

As you read, consider the following questions:

1. What evidence does Obama say shows that Assad used chemical weapons on his own people?

2. What implications do Assad's actions have beyond the use of chemical weapons, according to Obama?

Barack Obama, "Statement by the President on Syria," White House, August 31, 2013.

3. On what does the author say that the rights of individuals depend?

Ten days ago [August 21, 2013], the world watched in horror as men, women and children were massacred in Syria in the worst chemical weapons attack of the 21st century. Yesterday the United States presented a powerful case that the Syrian government was responsible for this attack on its own people.

Our intelligence shows the [Bashar al-]Assad regime and its forces preparing to use chemical weapons, launching rockets in the highly populated suburbs of Damascus, and acknowledging that a chemical weapons attack took place. And all of this corroborates what the world can plainly see—hospitals overflowing with victims; terrible images of the dead. All told, well over 1,000 people were murdered. Several hundred of them were children—young girls and boys gassed to death by their own government.

This attack is an assault on human dignity. It also presents a serious danger to our national security. It risks making a mockery of the global prohibition on the use of chemical weapons. It endangers our friends and our partners along Syria's borders, including Israel, Jordan, Turkey, Lebanon and Iraq. It could lead to escalating use of chemical weapons, or their proliferation to terrorist groups who would do our people harm.

In a world with many dangers, this menace must be confronted.

Now, after careful deliberation, I have decided that the United States should take military action against Syrian regime targets. This would not be an open-ended intervention. We would not put boots on the ground. Instead, our action would be designed to be limited in duration and scope. But I'm confident we can hold the Assad regime accountable for their use of chemical weapons, deter this kind of behavior, and degrade their capacity to carry it out.

Our military has positioned assets in the region. The Chairman of the Joint Chiefs has informed me that we are prepared to strike whenever we choose. Moreover, the Chairman has indicated to me that our capacity to execute this mission is not time-sensitive; it will be effective tomorrow, or next week, or one month from now. And I'm prepared to give that order.

Congressional Approval

But having made my decision as Commander-in-Chief based on what I am convinced is our national security interests, I'm also mindful that I'm the President of the world's oldest constitutional democracy. I've long believed that our power is rooted not just in our military might, but in our example as a government of the people, by the people, and for the people. And that's why I've made a second decision: I will seek authorization for the use of force from the American people's representatives in Congress.

Over the last several days, we've heard from members of Congress who want their voices to be heard. I absolutely agree. So this morning, I spoke with all four congressional leaders, and they've agreed to schedule a debate and then a vote as soon as Congress comes back into session.

In the coming days, my administration stands ready to provide every member with the information they need to understand what happened in Syria and why it has such profound implications for America's national security. And all of us should be accountable as we move forward, and that can only be accomplished with a vote.

I'm confident in the case our government has made without waiting for U.N. inspectors. I'm comfortable going forward without the approval of a United Nations Security Council that, so far, has been completely paralyzed and unwilling to hold Assad accountable. As a consequence, many people have advised against taking this decision to Congress, and undoubtedly, they were impacted by what we saw happen in the United Kingdom this week when the Parliament of our closest ally failed to pass a resolution with a similar goal, even as the Prime Minister supported taking action.

Yet, while I believe I have the authority to carry out this military action without specific congressional authorization, I know that the country will be stronger if we take this course, and our actions will be even more effective. We should have this debate, because the issues are too big for business as usual. And this morning [House Speaker] John Boehner, [Senate majority leader] Harry Reid, [House minority leader] Nancy Pelosi and [Senate minority leader] Mitch McConnell agreed that this is the right thing to do for our democracy.

A country faces few decisions as grave as using military force, even when that force is limited. I respect the views of those who call for caution, particularly as our country emerges from a time of war that I was elected in part to end. But if we really do want to turn away from taking appropriate action in the face of such an unspeakable outrage, then we must acknowledge the costs of doing nothing.

Values Must Be Enforced

Here's my question for every member of Congress and every member of the global community: What message will we send if a dictator can gas hundreds of children to death in plain sight and pay no price? What's the purpose of the international system that we've built if a prohibition on the use of chemical weapons that has been agreed to by the governments of 98 percent of the world's people and approved overwhelmingly by the Congress of the United States is not enforced?

Make no mistake—this has implications beyond chemical warfare. If we won't enforce accountability in the face of this heinous act, what does it say about our resolve to stand up to others who flout fundamental international rules? To governments who would choose to build nuclear arms? To terrorists who would spread biological weapons? To armies who carry out genocide?

We cannot raise our children in a world where we will not follow through on the things we say, the accords we sign, the values that define us.

So just as I will take this case to Congress, I will also deliver this message to the world. While the U.N. investigation has some time to report on its findings, we will insist that an atrocity committed with chemical weapons is not simply investigated, it must be confronted.

I don't expect every nation to agree with the decision we have made. Privately we've heard many expressions of support from our friends. But I will ask those who care about the writ of the international community to stand publicly behind our action.

And finally, let me say this to the American people: I know well that we are weary of war. We've ended one war in Iraq. We're ending another in Afghanistan. And the American people have the good sense to know we cannot resolve the underlying conflict in Syria with our military. In that part of the world, there are ancient sectarian differences, and the hopes of the Arab Spring have unleashed forces of change that are going to take many years to resolve. And that's why we're not contemplating putting our troops in the middle of someone else's war.

Instead, we'll continue to support the Syrian people through our pressure on the Assad regime, our commitment to the opposition, our care for the displaced, and our pursuit of a political resolution that achieves a government that respects the dignity of its people.

The International Order

But we are the United States of America, and we cannot and must not turn a blind eye to what happened in Damascus.

Secretary of State Kerry on the Threat of Syria

Now, to those who doubt whether Assad's actions have to have consequences, remember that our inaction absolutely is guaranteed to bring worse consequences. You, every one of you here—we, all of us—America will face this. If not today, somewhere down the line when the permissiveness of not acting now gives Assad license to go do what he wants—and threaten Israel, threaten Jordan, threaten Lebanon, create greater instability in a region already wracked by instability, where stability is one of the greatest priorities of our foreign policy and of our national security interest.

And that brings me to the second question that I've heard lately, which is sort of: What's really at stake here? Does this really affect us? I met earlier today with [Ohio congressman] Steve Chabot and had a good conversation. I asked him, "What are you hearing?" I know what you're all hearing. The instant reaction of a lot of Americans anywhere in our country is, "Whoa, we don't want to go to war again. We don't want to go to Iraq. We don't want to go to Afghanistan. We've seen how those turned out." I get it. . . .

But I want to make it clear at the outset, as each of us at this table want to make it clear, that what Assad has done directly affects America's security—America's security. We have a huge national interest in containing all weapons of mass destruction. And the use of gas is a weapon of mass destruction. Allowing those weapons to be used with impunity would be an enormous chink in our armor that we have built up over years against proliferation.

John Kerry, "Opening Remarks Before the House Armed Services Committee," September 16, 2013.

Out of the ashes of world war, we built an international order and enforced the rules that gave it meaning. And we did so because we believe that the rights of individuals to live in peace and dignity depends on the responsibilities of nations. We aren't perfect, but this nation more than any other has been willing to meet those responsibilities.

So to all members of Congress of both parties, I ask you to take this vote for our national security. I am looking forward to the debate. And in doing so, I ask you, members of Congress, to consider that some things are more important than partisan differences or the politics of the moment.

Ultimately, this is not about who occupies this office at any given time; it's about who we are as a country. I believe that the people's representatives must be invested in what America does abroad, and now is the time to show the world that America keeps our commitments. We do what we say. And we lead with the belief that right makes might—not the other way around.

We all know there are no easy options. But I wasn't elected to avoid hard decisions. And neither were the members of the House and the Senate. I've told you what I believe, that our security and our values demand that we cannot turn away from the massacre of countless civilians with chemical weapons. And our democracy is stronger when the President and the people's representatives stand together.

I'm ready to act in the face of this outrage. Today I'm asking Congress to send a message to the world that we are ready to move forward together as one nation.

"*Far from advancing U.S. security, getting involved in Syria would ensnare
Americans in a completely unnecessary
conflict.*"

Should America
Enter Syria's Hell?

Doug Bandow

*Doug Bandow is a senior fellow at the Cato Institute and a
former special assistant to President Ronald Reagan. In the following viewpoint, he argues that Syria is not a threat to the
United States and that America cannot solve the Syrian civil
war. He adds that the Middle East is a mass of conflict and that
Syria's use of chemical weapons will not substantially destabilize
the region. He also argues that chemical weapons are not true
weapons of mass destruction and that defending American credibility is not a good reason to go to war. He concludes that the
United States should stay out of the Syrian conflict.*

As you read, consider the following questions:

1. According to Bandow, what was President Ronald
   Reagan's greatest mistake?

2. Why does the author argue that Assad would not target a US ally?

3. What arguments does Bandow use to show that the focus on chemical weapons is misguided?

On Saturday President Barack Obama surprised most everyone in America by making the right decision and asking Congress for authority to go to war in Syria. Now Congress should make the right decision and vote no.

One of the impacts of being a superpower is that America has interests everywhere. However, most of those interests are modest, even peripheral. Conflicts and crises abound around the globe, but few significantly impact U.S. security. So it is with Syria.

The bitter civil war obviously is a human tragedy. However, the conflict is beyond repair by Washington.

Ronald Reagan's greatest mistake was getting involved in the Lebanese civil war, which at one point contained 25 warring factions. The U.S. invasion of Iraq sparked civil conflict which killed tens or even hundreds of thousands of civilians. Allied intervention in Libya prolonged that brutal low-tech battle and left terrorism and instability in its wake. Egypt, where America has successively backed dictatorship, democracy, and military rule, seems headed towards growing violent conflict, with the possibility of terrorism and even civil war.

Civil wars are particularly resistant to outside solution. The antagonisms run deep and there often are multiple parties, none of whom may want peace. In Syria the radical Islamists appear to be gaining influence. It is not obvious how the same government officials who have made such a mess of so many other countries would fix Syria.

Nor would the fighting likely end even if the U.S. ousted the Assad regime. Insurgent factions then likely would fight for dominance of either the whole of Syria or breakaway regions. For many rebels, revenge against those backing the regime, as well as members of groups noted for their support, such as Alawites[1] and Christians, would become a top priority. Then the U.S. would have to intervene again—or ignore the bloodletting, as it did in Kosovo when ethnic Albanians exacted retribution.[2]

Even if nation-building in Syria wasn't such a daunting task, the U.S. government should not risk the lives of its citizens in conflicts where Americans have no substantial stake. Policymakers have no warrant to be generous with fellow citizens' lives. Protecting this nation, its territory, people, liberty, and prosperity, remains the highest duty for Washington.

Far from advancing U.S. security, getting involved in Syria would ensnare Americans in a completely unnecessary conflict. Damascus has neither the ability nor the interest to attack the U.S. Any attempt by the Assad government to strike, including with chemical weapons, would trigger massive retaliation—perhaps even with nuclear weapons, which are true weapons of mass destruction.

While the Assad regime theoretically could target a U.S. ally, it has no incentive to do so. After all, its very survival remains threatened by a determined insurgent challenge. Israel, Saudi Arabia, and Turkey all are well heeled and well armed. All are capable of deterring attack.

The administration implausibly claims that striking the Syrian government would help protect Israel. However, President Bashar al-Assad is not suicidal, which he would be to attack Israel. Damascus did not even retaliate against Israel for destroying an apparent nuclear reactor. But Israel would be at risk if the Assad regime dissolves and insurgents, including radical Islamists, gained control of chemical weapon stockpiles. A more likely beneficiary of U.S. firepower would be

1. A denomination of Shia Islam.
2. The United States intervened against the Serbians on behalf of Kosovo Albanians in 1999, allowing the Albanians to wreak genocidal vengeance upon the remaining Serbian population.

Saudi Arabia, which has done more than any other nation to promote fundamental Islamic theology around the globe.

Some war advocates hope that hitting Damascus would weaken Iran. However, the administration has emphasized that it does not intend to actually weaken the Assad regime, making the attack a nearly purposeless gesture. Moreover, to the extent that Iran feels more isolated, it may press for tighter ties with Shia-dominated Iraq, which faces an increasing challenge from militant Sunnis. Tehran's divided elites also likely would close ranks against any possible peaceful deal over its nuclear program, which would be the regime's only sure guarantee of survival.

The Syrian conflict is destabilizing, but the Mideast never has been at rest. Most of the countries are artificial, created by British and French line-drawing a century ago. Most of the Arab states have been run by kleptocratic dictators, generals, and monarchs. Revolution has swept Egypt, Iran, Libya, and Tunisia while protests have shaken Bahrain. Iraq and Turkey confronted lengthy Kurdish insurgencies. Jordan forcibly suppressed Palestinian forces.

War consumed Libya and united two Yemens into one, which now could fall apart. Lebanon dissolved into years of civil war and recovered, but is threatened by [radical Islamist militant group] Hezbollah's dominant role. Iraq attacked Iran and conquered Kuwait, only to lose to a U.S.-led coalition [in the 1991 First Gulf War]. Later occupied by the U.S., Iraq dissolved into bitter internal conflict and now seems headed back in that direction. Israel has faced multiple wars with multiple opponents as well as resistance in the occupied territories.

And people worry about Syria destabilizing the Middle East?

The entire focus on chemical weapons is misguided. The travesty of the Syrian civil war is that more than 100,000 people apparently have died, not that some were killed with chemical weapons. The latter are not really weapons of mass

The Middle East

destruction. They are difficult to deploy and not so deadly. Explained John Mueller of Ohio State University, in World War I "it took over a ton of gas to produce a single fatality. Only about two or three percent of those gassed on the Western front died. By contrast, wounds from a traditional weapon proved 10 to 12 times more likely to be fatal." At least 99 percent of the millions of battlefield deaths in that conflict were caused by other means. Banning the weapon that killed one percent while ignoring the weapons which killed the other 99 percent exhibited a strange moral sense.

Entering yet another war against a Muslim nation in the Middle East is bound to create more enemies for America. The surest way to encourage future terrorists is to join other nations' conflicts and kill other nations' peoples. Washington is still fighting a traditional war in Afghanistan and "drone wars" in Pakistan and Yemen. The U.S. should avoid adding another conflict to the mix. It doesn't matter whether Americans believe their actions to be justified. Those on the receiving end of U.S. weapons would believe otherwise.

Even if the administration is genuinely committed to only minor military action, Washington would find it hard to be only half in. The more limited the strikes, the less likely they are to achieve anything other than suggest the pretense of enforcement of the president's "red line." But even inconsequential missile attacks would represent increased U.S. investment in the Syrian civil war. Pressure on Washington to do more would steadily grow, with a warlike Greek Chorus intoning "U.S. credibility" at every turn.

However, concern over credibility does not warrant making a bad decision to enter an unnecessary war. American presidents routinely put U.S. credibility on the line without backing up their threats—how many times have we heard that North Korea cannot be allowed to possess nuclear weapons? However, the only policy worse than tolerating a North Korean nuclear weapon would be bombing [its capital] Pyongyang.

The real lesson of President Obama's throwaway comment on Syrian chemical weapons is that red lines should not be drawn unless they reflect overriding, even vital interests and are worth war to enforce. Other nations will respect American demands if Washington rarely issues ultimatums, and only for obviously core interests. Going to war for minimal, even frivolous stakes to enhance credibility is a fool's bargain.

The president has placed the decision whether to go to war where it belongs, with Congress. Legislators should act on behalf of the American people, not the Obama administration. And the right decision is to keep the U.S. at peace.

Britain's House of Commons has shown the way. After members rejected the government's war policy, Prime Minister David Cameron observed: "it is clear to me that the British parliament, reflecting the views of the British people, does not want to see British military action. I get that and the government will act accordingly."

President Obama needs to "get that" and his government needs to "act accordingly."

Syria is a tragedy. But it is not America's tragedy. Legislators should reject war with Syria.

*"[The United States] should use mili-
tary cyber weapons [against Syria] . . .
to show that cyber operations are not
evil witchcraft but can be humanitarian."*

Why the U.S. Should Use Cyber Weapons Against Syria

Jason Healey

*Jason Healey is the director of the Cyber Statecraft Initiative at
the Atlantic Council of the United States and editor of* A Fierce
Domain: Cyber Conflict, 1986 to 2012. *In the following viewpoint, he argues that the United States should use cyber weapons
in an assault on Syria. Specifically, he contends that an American cyber attack could damage Syrian air defenses in preparation for a strike or could be used to damage Syrian chemical
weapons capability. Such attacks, Healey maintains, would be a
humanitarian way to damage Syria while limiting loss of life
and could show the world that US cyber weapons are a force for
good.*

As you read, consider the following questions:

1. According to Healey, why did the Treasury Department and senior political officials refuse to use cyber weapons against Slobodan Milosevic and Saddam Hussein?

2. Why does the author say that US cyber weapons have been seen as a force for evil?

3. Why does Healey think that the United States will probably not use cyber weapons?

If the [Barack] Obama administration does conduct military strikes against Syria, as seems likely, it should use military cyber weapons at the earliest possible moment to show the upside of military cyber power. Though this is risky, as it puts the focus on the U.S. militarization of cyberspace, it is likely worth doing to show that cyber operations are not evil witchcraft but can be humanitarian.

The Case of Serbia

This is not the first time the United States has been here. In 1999, the White House was reported to have initially approved a plan for covert "computer attacks on foreign bank accounts held by [Slobodan] Milosevic and other Serbian leaders, such as draining assets or altering banking records." A few years later, during the time of the second invasion of Iraq, a similar plan was rolled out to "cripple" the financial system of Saddam Hussein's Iraq, leaving him "no money for war supplies. No money to pay troops."

Neither plan seems to have been executed. The Treasury Department and senior political officials apparently blocked these attacks, for fear of cascading failures and setting a precedent of targeting banks.

A Cyber Strike on Libya Called Off

More recently, according to the *New York Times*, the Obama administration and military commanders considered "a cyber-offensive to disrupt and even disable the [Libyan dictator Muammar] Gaddafi government's air-defense system." A cyber strike on Libya was apparently ruled out both because there was not enough time and also because officials felt that cyber capabilities are like a "Ferrari" which should be saved for the "big race." The Israeli Air Force apparently did not think so, as it was widely reported they used a backdoor "kill switch" to disable Syrian air defenses en route to destroying an illicit nuclear reactor.

Given this history, what can and should the United States do today against Syria?

The Syrian Situation

It is unlikely that President Obama will authorize covert cyber operations against Bashar Assad's finances. Both of his immediate predecessors declined such attacks and the world economy and financial sector are already in a perilous state. A limited cyber attack integrated with traditional military forces should be a far more tempting option.

Cyber capabilities could first disrupt Syrian air defenses directly or confuse military command and control, allowing air strikes to proceed unchallenged. A cyber strike might also disable dual-use Syrian critical infrastructure (such as electrical power) that aids the regime's military but with no long-term destruction as would be caused by traditional bombs. Last, it is possible the U.S. military has cyber capabilities to directly disrupt the operations of Syria's chemical troops. This would need very specific capabilities against hard-to-reach computers; any disruption would be short but such an attack is feasible.

The first constraint which reportedly ruled out cyber attacks against Libyan air defenses, the time needed, should not be a constraint for Syria: the U.S. military has had months if not years to develop the requisite cyber capabilities along with options to deliver them to the optimal targets.

The Stuxnet Worm

On the second constraint, this might be the 'big race' that U.S. officials have been waiting for, but for political reasons, rather than military. In the past several years, the United States has been caught using Stuxnet [a computer worm] to conduct a covert cyber campaign against Iran as well as trawling the Internet with the massive PRISM [data] collection operation. The world is increasingly seeing U.S. cyber power as a force for evil in the world.

A cyber operation against Syria might help to reverse this view.

Recently, experts from the United States, China, Russia and other states reported to the U.N. Secretary General that existing international law, including international humanitarian law (aka, the laws of armed conflict such as the Geneva and Hague conventions) apply to cyber conflict. By sparing the lives of Syrian troops and nearby civilians, an opening cyber operation against Syria could demonstrate exactly how such capabilities can be compliant with international humanitarian law. European allies would see an operation within the norms of shared transatlantic principles, not at odds with them like Stuxnet or PRISM.

A Self-Sustaining Taboo

Unfortunately, it is unlikely cyber capabilities will be used, or at least unlikely the White House and military will discuss them even if they are. The classification around these operations has created a self-sustaining taboo. Even though the U.S. national interest is greatly served by removing the voodoo mystique around them, official silence will allow doubters and the ill-informed to continue to dominate the debate.

Despite my own background in U.S. military offensive and defensive cyber operations, I have long been a skeptic of the use of military cyber power as it has been used off the battlefield in sneaky circumstances. America should take this chance

Stuxnet and Iran

Iran has apparently suffered the most attacks by the Stuxnet worm and ... may well have been its main target. A September 2010 study by [computer security firm] Symantec argued that the "concentration of infections in Iran likely indicates that this was the initial target for infections and was where infections were initially seeded." As of September 25, 2010, Iran had identified "the IP addresses of 30,000 industrial computer systems" that had been infected by Stuxnet, according to Mahmoud Liaii, director of the Information Technology Council of Iran's Industries and Mines Ministry, who argued that the virus "is designed to transfer data about production lines from our industrial plants" to locations outside of Iran.

Iranian officials have indicated that the worm infected computers associated with the country's nuclear power plant under construction near Bushehr. Dr. Mohammad Ahmadian, an Iranian Atomic Energy Organization official, stated in October that the worm may have been transferred to computers at the reactor site via "CDs and Flash memory sticks," adding that the affected computers have since been "inspected and cleaned up." Some of those responsible for transferring the worm were "foreign experts who had been frequenting industrial centres," Iran's minister of communication Reza Taqipur stated in October [2010]. Iranian officials have indicated that the reactor, which is not yet operational, has not been affected by Stuxnet....

In addition to Liaii's description of Stuxnet's purpose, reports of the Stuxnet infections in Iran have, as noted, fueled speculation that the virus was part of an effort by some countries, including the United States and Israel, to sabotage Tehran's nuclear programs.

Paul K. Kerr, John Rollins, and Catherine A. Theohary,
Congressional Research Service, December 9, 2010.

to demystify these weapons to show the world they, and the U.S. military in general, can be used on the battlefield in line with humanitarian principles.

"The situation in Syria ... means arming people, many of whom we don't like and who don't like us, to reduce the likelihood of a dangerous increase in the power of people who consider themselves at war with us."

The United States Should Arm Syrian Rebels

Walter Russell Mead

Walter Russell Mead is James Clarke Chace Professor of Foreign Affairs and Humanities at Bard College in New York and editor at large of the American Interest *magazine. In the following viewpoint he argues that the United States should provide arms to moderate Syrian rebel groups. Mead notes that he does not expect these groups to win or establish a democratic or US-friendly Syrian government, but they could deter the establishment of a possible al Qaeda–affiliated radical Islamist government if Assad is deposed, which would spread chaos throughout the region and increase terrorism. He says that giving weapons to moderate rebel groups is a way to prevent such a worst-case scenario and is thus the best of the many bad options confronting the United States regarding the Syrian issue.*

As you read, consider the following questions:

1. According to Mead, what probable policies of a new Syrian government will the United States dislike?

2. What does the author say is the worst case for the United States in a post-Assad Syria?

3. What does Mead say distracted the United States from the conflict in Libya?

Greg Scoblete at RCW [RealClearWorld] takes us to task for advocating arming a faction among the Syrian militia as an advisable course of action:

> This is a common lament, both among pro-interventionist Western commentators and among Syrian rebel forces themselves. But how true is it? Let's presume the U.S. arms the rebels—but only the Good Ones Who Share Our Values—and they're able to fight more effectively against [Bashar] Assad's forces. Will the jihadists decide to quit the battlefield? Why would they do that? Are we supposed to assume that the Syrian forces fighting the Assad regime will instantly turn their guns on the jihadists in their midst if and when they succeed in overthrowing Assad? Won't they have bigger fish to fry at that point?

The Post-Assad Syrian Government

These are valid concerns. U.S. support for rebels in Syria is very unlikely to produce a post-war Syrian government that we like. In fact, what we need to understand in all of this that we aren't going to like the new Syrian government very much. It's probably going to be less free, more anti-Israel, and significantly more Islamist than we would want. It's likely that there will be revenge killings and even bloodbaths along the way.

Syria is a lot like Lebanon's bigger, uglier, and meaner brother. The ethnic and religious tensions that produced decades of civil war in Lebanon are also present in Syria. The Assad dictatorship imposed a rigid order on Syria, but as the dictatorship crumbles the divisions are coming back into public view. Unless we were willing to put tens, maybe hundreds of thousands of troops in Syria and keep them there for a long time, often fighting bad guys and getting attacked by suicide bombers, we don't stand much chance of building an orderly and stable society there, much less an open and free one.

I don't think the United States has the will to do this right now, and beyond pure humanitarian grounds it is hard to see that such a course would serve the national interest. However, even if our Syria policy isn't about achieving something good, we should still be thinking about what we can do that reduces the chances of things getting catastrophically worse.

Al-Qaeda in Syria

The worst case for the United States in a post-Assad Syria would be that groups linked to al-Qaeda become dominant players either in the country's government as a whole or in control of significant regions in a country that fragments. Such groups would be nests of terrorists acting to destabilize not only Syria itself but Iraq, Lebanon, and the wider Middle East. They would certainly be active in Russia and, through extensive ties with the Arab diaspora in Europe, add considerably to the security headaches the West faces. They would be actively working to destabilize governments across the Arab world as well and providing shelter, training, and arms to terrorists from all over. In a worst, worst case scenario, they get hold of Assad's WMD [weapons of mass destruction] stockpiles and start passing them out to their friends.

The United States does not want any of this to happen. We could not long stand idly by if it did.

Aiding the less ugly, less bad guys in the Syrian resistance, and even finding a few actual good guys to support, isn't about installing a pro-American government in post civil war

Syria. It's about minimizing the prospects for a worst-case scenario—by shortening the era of conflict and so, hopefully, reducing the radicalization of the population and limiting the prospects that Syrian society as a whole will descend into all-out chaotic massacres and civil conflict. And it's about making sure that other people in Syria, unsavory on other grounds as they may be, who don't like al-Qaeda type groups and don't want them to establish a permanent presence in the country, have enough guns and ammunition to get their way.

This is not a plan to edge the United States toward military engagement in Syria; it is aimed at reducing the chance that American forces will need to get involved. And, by accelerating the overthrow of Assad, it's also a strategy for putting more pressure on Iran, pressure that represents our best hope of avoiding war with the mullahs [Iranian clergy who govern that country] as well. The whole point here is to keep our troops at home.

Preventing the Worst Case

If the United States hadn't gotten itself distracted by the ill-considered intervention in Libya [in 2011], we might have acted in Syria at an earlier stage, when there were some better options on the table. But we are past that now; the White House humanitarians did what humanitarians often do—inadvertently promoting a worse disaster in one place (in this case, Syria) by failing to integrate their humanitarian impulses (in Libya) with strategic reflection. This kind of strategic incompetence is the greatest single flaw in the humanitarian approach to foreign policy. It has led to untold misery in the past and will likely lead to many more bloodbaths in the future. Unfortunately, warm hearted fuzzy brained humanitarianism is one of the world's greatest killers.

The situation in Syria now isn't about doing good or preventing bloodbaths. The bloodbath is here and there is not a lot of good that can be done within the range of our capacity and will. This is now all about trying to prevent the worst rather than promoting the best. It means arming people, many of whom we don't like and who don't like us, to reduce the likelihood of a dangerous increase in the power of people who consider themselves at war with us and our friends.

One option people are talking about is to assist defected Syrian officers in a military council to oversee the rebels. Manaf Tlass and his colleagues might be able to establish some kind of unified command that could funnel weapons from the Gulf to certain rebel brigades, marginalize the terrorists, and, if Assad falls, maintain some semblance of order to prevent even worse chaos and bloodbath from erupting across the country. We don't have the intel here at *Via Meadia* that would let us judge whether Tlass and company are our best bet—but something like this may need to be tried.

There is nothing nice or pretty about this, and we don't expect much good to come out of it. But bad policy decisions in the past combine with the increasingly dangerous situation on the ground to paint us in a corner where we don't have much choice.

> "The worst thing that America and the rest of the world could do is to arm the opposition [in Syria]."

Don't Arm Syria's Rebels

Gary Kamiya

Gary Kamiya is a cofounder of Salon, *a well-known online magazine. In the following viewpoint, he argues that arming the Syrian rebels will only prolong the Iraq war and cause more death and havoc. He contends that the best possible outcome in Syria is probably for Assad to remain in power while offering some political concessions, and for the war to end quickly. America, he maintains, is reluctant to admit that there are some disasters it cannot avert, but it must recognize this if it is not to create even greater tragedies.*

As you read, consider the following questions:

1. According to Kamiya, what is the only way that Assad could lose the war?

2. As stated by the author, why does the International Crisis Group say that America's strategy of arming the opposition while pursuing diplomacy will not work?

Gary Kamiya, "Don't Arm Syria's Rebels," *Salon*, April 13, 2012. Copyright © 2012 by Salon. This article first appeared in Salon.com, at http://www.Salon.com. An online version remains in the Salon archives. Reprinted with permission.

3. What bad foreign policy decisions does Kamiya attribute to American optimism?

In Syria, the horror has taken a brief break. The [UN secretary-general] Kofi Annan–brokered cease-fire is holding so far, give or take a few government snipers, but no one expects it to last. Within hours, days or weeks, something will break the fragile calm. President Bashar al-Assad's tanks will once again begin firing high-explosive shells into civilian neighborhoods, blowing up houses and everyone in them. Opposition fighters will kill government troops and set off bombs. Mysterious massacres, which each side will blame on the other, will take place. Soldiers will continue to rape women, children will be tortured, and the horrible human toll—9,000 deaths, 42,000 refugees since fighting began 13 months ago [in March 2011]—will continue to climb.

There is a very good chance that this slow-motion blood bath could go on for years. And at the end, Assad could still be in power.

As this dreadful situation festers, calls for America to arm the opposition are growing louder. And they are not only coming from neocons, neo-imperialists and warmongers, proxy warriors for whom defeating Assad is part of a Great Game whose real goal is defeating Iran. No one is surprised that neocons like [US senator] Joe Lieberman, for whom America's foreign policy comes down to "Is it good for Israel?" or his chest-beating partner in imperialist Islamophobia, [Republican senator] John McCain, want the U.S. to arm the Syrian opposition. Nor is it surprising that [American diplomat] Elliott Abrams, Fox News or the *Washington Post* editorial board have beat the war drums. But these predictable hawks have been joined by an increasing number of liberals and humanitarians who have no ideological ax to grind.

Saying "the basis for any settlement must be a rough equality of forces," *New York Times* columnist Roger Cohen called for the U.S. to arm the Syrian opposition. Analyst James Traub similarly called for the U.S. to back what he called a "neo-mujahadeen strategy." *Guardian* columnist Simon Tisdall blasted [President Barack] Obama's refusal to get the U.S. more involved, saying that the world had a "moral imperative" to intervene. "A shoulder shrug will just not cut it any more," Tisdall wrote. In a column titled "Syria is not Iraq. And it is not always wrong to intervene," Tisdall's *Guardian* colleague Jonathan Freedland denounced facile left-wing opposition to Western intervention in Syria, writing, "we must not make the people of Horns pay the price for the mistake we made in Baghdad." Oxford economist Paul Collier argued in the *Financial Times* that Assad's regime was doomed and arming the opposition would push it over the edge.

None of these commentators are neoconservatives or proxy warriors, fans of the "War on Terror," the [George W.] Bush Doctrine [that the USA has the right to attack other countries to secure itself] or the unbridled use of American force. In their different ways, they are driven by simple, and legitimate, moral outrage. That outrage was expressed in its purest form by the Iraqi exile Kanan Makiya, the Iraqi exile whose powerful indictment of [executed Iraqi dictator] Saddam Hussein's tyranny played a large role in convincing liberals like [American journalist and author] George Packer and [American journalist and author] Paul Berman to support the Iraq War. In a largely pro-intervention symposium posted recently by the *New Republic*, Makiya wrote, "I don't really think there is any kind of a reasonable argument against intervention in Syria. Quite the opposite: There is a moral and a human imperative to act that is larger than any nation's interests and larger than any strategic calculation. That is so obvious it is an embarrassment to have to say it. This is how I thought about intervention in Iraq 20 years ago and it is how I think about what needs to be done in Syria today."

To their credit, most of these observers recognize that their call for the West in general and America in particular to support the Syrian opposition holds considerable risks. For example, after acknowledging the murky and disorganized nature of the Syrian opposition, the looming possibility of sectarian massacres, and the unhappy outcome of America's mujahedin experiment in Afghanistan, Traub writes, "[T]here are no good solutions; only less bad ones . . . I'm open to a better suggestion."

So these commentators deserve respect for their intellectual integrity, their good intentions and their moral outrage. All of them find the unfolding carnage in Syria unbearable to behold, and anyone with a conscience would agree.

And yet, we must bear it. For the worst thing that America and the rest of the world could do is to arm the opposition.

This is not a knee-jerk left-wing response. It has nothing to do with Iraq. Nor does it have anything to do with the proxy war between the U.S. and its allies and Iran and its allies. It is not driven by pacifism or opposition to all war. All U.S. wars are not axiomatically foolish, evil or driven by brutal self-interest (although most of them since World War II have been). The airstrikes on Kosovo [in 1999] and the [2011] Libya campaign were justified (although the jury is still out on the latter intervention). If arming the Syrian opposition would result in fewer deaths and a faster transition to a peaceful, open, democratic society, we should arm them.

Every situation is different: There is no one-size-fits-all template for foreign affairs. And in Syria, the truth is that further militarizing the conflict will likely cause it to spiral out of control. Moral outrage alone is not enough. It must be tethered to a coldly rational analysis.

That analysis has been provided by a number of in-depth reports, most notably a new study by the International Crisis Group [ICG], as well as the excellent on-the-ground reporting of Nir Rosen for [Arabic news network] Al-Jazeera. The bottom line is simple. The war has become a zero-sum game for Assad. If he loses, he dies. But the only way he can lose is if he is abandoned by his crucial external patron, Russia, which is extremely unlikely to happen absent some slaughter so egregious that Moscow feels it has to cut ties with him. Assad has sufficient domestic support to hold on for a long time, and a huge army that is not likely to defect en masse. Under these circumstances, giving arms to the rebels, however much it may make conscience-stricken Western observers feel better, will simply make the civil war much bloodier and its outcome even more chaotic and dangerous.

The key point concerns Assad's domestic support. Contrary to the widely held belief that most Syrians support the opposition and are opposed to the Assad regime, Syrians are in fact deeply divided. The country's minorities—the ruling Alawites, Christians and Druze—tend to support the regime, if only because they fear what will follow its downfall. (The grocery on my corner in San Francisco is owned by a Christian Syrian from a village outside Damascus. When I asked him what he thought about what was going on in his country, he said, "It's not like what you see on TV. Assad is a nice guy. He's trying to do the right thing.") As Rosen makes clear, Syria's ruling Alawite minority is the key to Assad's survival: Absent an outside invasion, the regime will not fall unless the Alawites turn on it. But the Alawites fear reprisals if the Sunni-dominated opposition, some of whose members have threatened to "exterminate the Alawites," defeats the Assad regime. The fear of a sectarian war, exacerbated by the murky and incoherent nature of the opposition, means that the minorities are unlikely to join the opposition in large numbers. As for the opposition, it has suffered too many losses to stop fighting.

What this means is that neither side has any reason to stop pursuing its present course, and short of a U.S. or NATO [North Atlantic Treaty Organization] invasion—which only barking-mad neocons are suggesting we embark on—the regime will be able to hold on for years. The longer the struggle goes on, Rosen notes, the more radicalized and Islamist the opposition will become. As Rosen gloomily writes, "Syria is crumbling before our eyes, and a thoroughly modern nation is likely to be set back many decades."

The International Crisis Group report argues that America's current posture of talking about arming the opposition while simultaneously pursuing a diplomatic track is a mistake.

"In the meantime this dual U.S. and Arab approach—on the one hand, proclaiming support for Annan and for a diplomatic resolution; on the other, toying with greater militarization of the opposition—arguably is a strategy at war with itself and one that could readily backfire. Some argue that only by dangling the prospect of a stronger rebel force might Assad be persuaded to give in. But a different scenario is more likely: The regime will point to any decision to arm the opposition as a breach of the Annan plan and use it as a reason not to comply and to reinvigorate its own offensive; meanwhile, the military half-measures on behalf of the opposition might satisfy the urge to 'do something'—but these will be woefully inadequate to beat back a regime offensive." The ICG report recommends "a more pragmatic, consensual approach, a controlled, negotiated transition that would spare the country additional bloodshed . . . a middle course between chaos without the regime and chaos with it—a controlled transition that preserves state institutions, thoroughly reforms the security services and puts squarely on the table the issue of unaccountable family rule." To get there, it suggests strengthening some of mediator Kofi Annan's general ideas, including a monitoring mechanism to ensure that cease-fires are not violated, freezing of weapons smuggling across the border, and a pragmatic compromise on demonstrations that would allow them but not in the center of Damascus, where they would become [Egyptian] Tahrir Square–style mass movements that would topple the regime. In the long run, the radioactive issue of the Assad family's rule and legitimacy and the sectarian makeup of the security forces would have to be addressed. But in the short term, Assad would remain in power.

An Op-Ed piece in the *New York Times* by two law professors, Asli Bali and Aziz F. Rana, made the same point: The most humane thing for the Syrian people, the authors argue, would be to engage [diplomatically] with Assad—which means leaving him, at least for now, in power.

This means that the best-case scenario is that the fighting winds down, the opposition eventually gives up the armed struggle, contents itself with whatever crumbs Assad throws it, and waits for the political winds to shift enough so that real change can start taking place.

For this, thousands of men, women and children gave their lives?

Such an outcome seems morally outrageous. It's unthinkable. But the alternative—an all-out sectarian civil war between evenly matched adversaries, both of them fighting to the death—is even more unthinkable.

What America and the world are faced with in Syria, in short, is nothing less than a tragedy. And we are not good at dealing with tragedy.

Americans are not a tragic people. We do not understand tragedy, and we instinctively resist it. Our history has insulated us from it. American exceptionalism, the belief that we are qualitatively different from all other nations and immune to the woes that afflict them, goes back to the Puritans. No American president can avoid paying lip service to it. The Republican Party's foreign policy consists almost entirely of endless variations on it. It is in our national DNA.

The American belief that we live in a city on a hill, that we are immune from tragedy, has not only molded our national character, it has shaped our relations with the rest of the

The Syrian Civil War

In March of 2011 [Syrian] protesters, inspired by revolts in Egypt and Tunisia, held rallies in the south. Some protesters were shot and killed by security forces. Assad responded by firing his cabinet in April. Protests spread across Syria. Snipers fired on crowds, as did tanks sent to restore order. . . .

According to a United Nations (UN) report, some soldiers who refused to fire on unarmed civilians were executed. As the government continued to try to quell the uprising, President Barack Obama called for Assad's ouster. The United States instituted an investment embargo and the European Union agreed on an oil embargo. NATO took command of air strikes and patrols of the Mediterranean Sea, enforcing a UN arms embargo. . . . Throughout 2011 and 2012, many called for Assad to step down from power, including Turkish prime minister Recep Tayyip Erdogan. As of 2013, the violence continued in Syria, and Assad remained in power.

"Bashar al-Assad."
Gale Biography In Context, *2013.*

world. Some of its influence has been positive. Optimism and generosity, the benign face of American exceptionalism, drove epochal achievements like the Marshall Plan, which rebuilt a shattered Europe after World War II. That altruistic, engaged approach to the world known as "Wilsonian idealism" or "liberal interventionism" has resulted in some notable achievements, including the ouster of Serbian tyrant Slobodan Milosevic and the toppling of Libyan dictator Moammar Gadhafi. A foreign policy that does not have a moral component, a purely Machiavellian [politically unscrupulous and de-

53

ceptive] approach to the world, is soulless. Realism is essential, but realism without compassion is deadly.

But America's belief that it is inherently a force for good, that American interventions always have positive results, and that we can shape the world at will, have led us to make a number of appalling foreign policy decisions—ones that not only failed to advance our own interests, but that harmed the very people and causes we were allegedly trying to help. Vietnam and Afghanistan, our two longest wars, were both driven partly by altruistic motives—and both proved to be disastrous quagmires. George W. Bush's Iraq War was motivated by a bizarre mixture of factors—Zimmerman-style[1] vigilante vengeance for 9/11, a half-baked "grand strategy" to remake the Middle East for U.S. and Israel, a feckless and puerile president's desire to play the he-man—but lurking among them was a myopic, almost drugged belief that because we were the ones dropping the bombs, and God was on our side, everything was going to be OK in the end. Hundreds of thousands of dead Iraqis, thousands of dead American and coalition troops and a wrecked country later, everything did not turn out to be OK.

Our national instinct is to come riding to the rescue. It goes against our character to simply sit on our hands. Our sincere, naive and self-centered belief that America can fix everything, and our equally sincere, naive and self-centered belief that moral outrage justifies intervention, is a powerful tide, pulling us toward getting directly involved in Syria's civil war.

But in the real world, we cannot always come riding to the rescue. Sometimes, we have no choice but to watch tragedy unfold, because anything we do will create an even bigger tragedy.

---

1. Florida vigilante George Zimmerman shot and killed Trayvon Martin, an unarmed black teenager, in 2012.

America is going to have to come to terms with this painful truth, and a lot of similar ones, in the years ahead. We're going to have to accept that Obama's drone war is creating more enemies than it kills and shut it down, even if that means some potential terrorists get away. We're going to have to accept that Afghanistan and Iraq may end up as basket cases, even failed states. We're going to have to learn to live with an Egypt run by Islamists, and an Israeli-Palestinian conflict that can no longer be solved with a two-state solution. We're going to have to give up on the dream of perfect safety from terrorism.

After too many childish illusions, and childish wars that killed too many people, it's time for us to grow up.

> "*[Obama's asking congressional approval] will have force in rebalancing the allocation of authority between executive and legislative branches in the deployment of U.S. military assets.*"

Asking Congress to Approve Attacks on Syria Acknowledges Limits on the President's War Powers

Peter M. Shane

Peter M. Shane is the Jacob E. Davis and Jacob E. Davis II Chair in Law at the Ohio State University's Moritz College of Law. He is the author of Madison's Nightmare: Unchecked Executive Power and the Threat to American Democracy. *In the following viewpoint he asserts that presidents since World War II have generally used military force without consulting Congress. He maintains that President Barack Obama's decision to go to Congress for approval of military action in Syria sets an important precedent and will influence future debate about engaging in a war.*

Peter M. Shane, "Rebalancing War Powers: President Obama's Momentous Decision," *Shane Reactions,* September 1, 2013. www.shanereactions.wordpress.com. Copyright © 2013 by Peter M. Shane. All rights reserved. Reproduced by permission.

As you read, consider the following questions:

1. According to Shane, what is the "living Constitution" argument used to support the idea that presidents can unilaterally use military force?

2. In what way would intervention in Syria be different than other military actions, according to the author?

3. Why does Shane say that it is a good thing that congressional approval of war be bipartisan?

President Obama's pursuit of congressional authority for a Syrian strike operation is, to date, his single most important decision in reshaping the post-9/11 presidency.

He early foreswore torture and declared the U.S. bound by the Geneva Conventions in the war against al Qaeda. These orders, however, only institutionalized legal positions into which the Supreme Court had already pushed the [George W.] Bush Administration. Guantanamo [Bay, a prison for terrorists on a US base in Cuba], despite Obama's best efforts, is still open.

But seeking authorization for a military strike against Syria marks the first time that a modern-day president has taken the initiative to elicit legislative approval for a military action that, by the President's own reckoning, would neither be a prolonged, nor a boots-on-the-ground operation.

Historical Precedents

In announcing his decision, President Obama, like both Presidents Bush [George H.W. and George W.], declared that he possessed the constitutional authority to act unilaterally. He said he does not need Congress's approval in order to proceed.

But historical precedents have consequences. Whatever their formal legal views, the Bushes' decisions helped cement a consistent pattern: With the exception of Korea, the United

States has never engaged in a massive or prolonged military deployment without some form of explicit congressional sanction. A President acting unilaterally to start what is sometimes called "a real war" henceforth would probably be courting impeachment.

Since World War II, presidents (with the exception of [Dwight D.] Eisenhower) and their lawyers have consistently maintained that executive power encompasses unilateral presidential authority to deploy military force wherever the President thinks necessary to protect the national security of the United States. As well documented by Tulane law professor Stephen M. Griffin, however, presidents made no such ambitious claims prior to World War II. It was common for high public officials, including presidents, to say the contrary.

Arguments for Unilateral Action

The modern argument generally takes either of two forms. One, elaborated by the State Department during the Vietnam War, is a kind of "living Constitution" argument. There is scholarly consensus that the Constitution intended for the President to have the authority, without advance congressional approval, to repel sudden invasions. The State Department argued that, under modern conditions, threats to U.S. national security anywhere in the world could be as urgent as the threat of an invasion would have been in 1789. Hence, the allocation of war-making authorities should now be understood to give the President unilateral war-making power that matches the scope of modern threats.

The second form of argument is that unilateral presidential power to conduct at least those military operations that fall short of "real war" has been ratified by Congress's implicit acquiescence in presidential actions of just this sort. In other words, presidents have acted without Congress, and Congress has not barred the practice. The War Powers Resolution is sometimes argued as supporting this view because it effectively permits the President on his own initiative to commit armed forces to combat for up to 60 days.

Neither of these arguments is frivolous, but each departs notably from the original Constitution. Because the Constitution vests authority in Congress to issue "letters of marque and reprisal," it is evident that the framers supposed congressional authority necessary to the deployment of military force even on a small scale.

A version of the history-based argument is, however, at least technically reconcilable with the original understanding. Congress's acquiescence can be understood as a form of congressional authorization, which still remains a necessary legal precondition for any presidential military initiative.

The problem for Obama regarding Syria, however, is that—as scholars as different in political orientation as [conservative law professor] Jack Goldsmith and [liberal law professor] David Cole have pointed out—no historical precedent quite resembles the punitive strike that the President seeks to inflict. There is no imminent danger to U.S. persons or property. We are not acting at the behest of the sitting government. We would not be acting in pursuit of any resolution of the U.N. Security Council. It could not even be argued, as with Kosovo, [where the US bombed Serbian forces in 1999] that the strike was necessary to reaffirm the cohesiveness of NATO [North Atlantic Treaty Organization]. Proceeding without either clear domestic precedent or obvious defense under international law would come close to saying that the President's authority to deploy military force is beyond legal limit.

Presidential Accountability

In seeking congressional authorization, President Obama is thus re-submitting the modern presidency to the kind of "cycle of accountability," to use Professor Griffin's phrase, that the constitutional design anticipated. We will strike Syria, if at all,

2013 Polls Showing US Public Opposition to Syria Airstrikes

	Favor	Oppose	Unsure
Pew Research (Aug 29–Sep 1, n=1,000 adults): Would you favor or oppose the U.S. conducting military airstrikes against Syria in response to reports that the Syrian government used chemical weapons?	29%	48%	23%
Washington Post/ABC News (Aug 28–Sep 1, n=1,012 adults): The United States says it has determined that the Syrian government has used chemical weapons in the civil war there. Given this, do you support or oppose the United States launching missile strikes against the Syrian government?	36%	59%	5%
NBC News (Aug 28–29, n=700 adults): It has been reported that the Syrian government has used chemical weapons on its citizens. Do you think the United States should take military action against the Syrian government in response to the use of chemical weapons or not?	42%	50%	8%
Huffington Post/YouGov (Aug 26–27, n=1,000 adults online): Do you think the United States military should or should not use air strikes to aid rebels in Syria?	25%	41%	34%

TAKEN FROM: Ariel Edwards-Levy, "The American People Really Don't Want to Bomb Syria (Polls)," *Huffington Post*, September 3, 2013. www.huffingtonpost.com.

based on a joint determination by both elected branches that should nurture an ongoing sense of joint responsibility to monitor and assess in a careful way whatever consequences ensue.

It is all the better for this purpose that support for a resolution, if enacted, will necessarily be bipartisan. No party and no elected institution will be able to say, in the face of adverse consequences, "We didn't do this."

It is also a strategy under which the President accepts political risk. If Congress votes down a resolution that would authorize a strike action, the President might take the position that (a) failure to pass a resolution of authority does not equal the affirmative passage of a resolution denying him authority, and (b) absent the latter, he still has constitutional power to undertake the mission unilaterally. But it's not likely to be a politically viable argument. If Congress fails to authorize a Syria strike, the President is all but certain to desist—with obvious negative consequences for his credibility, both at home and abroad.

(It might be observed that no President who has gone to Congress for military authority has ever been turned down. But none has sought military authority from a legislative branch as polarized as the current Congress.)

Of course, historical precedents are not legal precedents like Supreme Court opinions. The norm of consistency across cases is not as strong in decision making where politics dominates.

But events, when they happen, exert a force on the future. Should President Obama or his successors seek to attack other nations in similar circumstances in the future—Iran, for example, to forestall its nuclear ambitions—the question will be asked, "Why can't Congress be involved, as it was in Syria?" This is an institutionally powerful question. It can limit the exertion of power. It will have force in rebalancing the allocation of authority between executive and legislative branches in the deployment of U.S. military assets in support of presidential foreign policy.

In the world of constitutional politics, this is a very big deal.

| "The war powers of the presidency remain as mighty as ever."

Obama Is Only Making His War Powers Mightier

Eric Posner

Eric Posner is Kirkland and Ellis Professor of Law at the University of Chicago Law School. In the following viewpoint, he discusses President Barack Obama's decision to seek support from Congress for air strikes on Syria and argues that Obama said that the congressional vote was optional and that the President has the right to order air strikes even if Congress disapproves. Posner contends that this reaffirms, rather than undermines, executive power. He maintains that Obama went to Congress for political reasons, not in order to rein in the power of the presidency.

As you read, consider the following questions:

1. What could the president have done that would have been worthy of notice in terms of war powers, according to Posner?

2. According to the author, what was Obama's motive in asking Congress for approval?

3. What reasons does Posner supply to show that Obama's legal rationale for an attack on Syria is weak?

President Obama's surprise announcement that he will ask Congress for approval of a military attack on Syria is being hailed as a vindication of the rule of law and a revival of the central role of Congress in war-making, even by critics. But all of this is wrong. Far from breaking new legal ground, President Obama has reaffirmed the primacy of the executive in matters of war and peace. The war powers of the presidency remain as mighty as ever.

It would have been different if the president had announced that only Congress can authorize the use of military force, as dictated by the Constitution, which gives Congress alone the power to declare war. *That* would have been worthy of notice, a reversal of the ascendance of executive power over Congress. But the president said no such thing. He said: "I believe I have the authority to carry out this military action without specific congressional authorization." Secretary of State John Kerry confirmed that the president "has the right to do that"—launch a military strike—"no matter what Congress does."

Thus, the president believes that the law gives him the *option* to seek a congressional yes or to act on his own. He does not believe that he is bound to do the first. He has merely stated the law as countless other presidents and their lawyers have described it before him.

The president's announcement should be understood as a political move, not a legal one. His motive is both self-serving and easy to understand, and it has been all but acknowledged by the administration. If Congress now approves the war, it must share blame with the president if what happens next in Syria goes badly. If Congress rejects the war, it must share blame with the president if [Syrian president] Bashar al-Assad gases more Syrian children. The big problem for Obama arises if Congress says no and he decides he must go ahead anyway, and *then* the war goes badly. He won't have broken the law as he understands it, but he will look bad. He would be the first president ever to ask Congress for the power to make war and then to go to war after Congress said no. (In the past, presidents who expected dissent did not ask Congress for permission.)

People who celebrate the president for humbly begging Congress for approval also apparently don't realize that his understanding of the law—that it gives him the option to go to Congress—maximizes executive power vis-à-vis Congress. If the president were required to act alone, without Congress, then he would have to take the blame for failing to use force when he should and using force when he shouldn't. If he were required to obtain congressional authorization, then Congress would be able to block him. But if he can have it either way, he can force Congress to share responsibility when he wants to and avoid it when he knows that it will stand in his way.

This approach also empowers the president relative to Congress by giving him the ability to embarrass members of Congress when he wants to. Just ask [former senator and presidential candidate] Hillary Clinton, whose vote in favor of the 2003 Iraq War damaged her chances against Barack Obama in 2008, and the Democratic senators who could not enter the 1992 campaign for the presidency because their votes against the 1991 Iraq War rendered them unelectable. The best thing for individual members of Congress is to be able to carp on the sidelines—to complain about not being consulted and to blame the president if the war goes badly. That is why [political consultant] David Axelrod said, "Congress is now the dog that caught the car." This is hardball politics, not a rediscovery of legal values.

If Obama gains by spreading blame among Congress, why didn't the president ask Congress for military authorization earlier, before he threatened Syria with a missile strike? The answer appears to be that the president expected international support for the invasion and believed that if other countries supported him, he would not need support in Congress. Only when the British poodle rediscovered its inner lion [that is, when normally obedient Great Britain disagreed with the United States] did he shift gears. Again, this has nothing to do with the law; it's a matter of political prudence.

And it is not hard to see why foreign countries refused to provide support. The legal rationale for the Syria intervention that the president fashioned—deterring the use of chemical weapons—has satisfied no other country. While no one likes chemical weapons, there is no reason to believe that the U.S. must deter their use by striking Syria. Iraq used chemical weapons 30 years ago, but no country followed its lead—even though no one bombed Iraq to punish it. Countries refrain from using chemical weapons because they inspire revulsion among people that governments usually need for support, not because there is a "norm" against them. And no matter how often Obama and Kerry say that they must intervene to enforce this norm, everyone understands that the real reason for U.S. intervention is to maintain the administration's credibility, or to ensure that the U.S. retains influence over events, or to give a psychological boost to moderate Syrian rebel groups—not to vindicate international law (which the U.S. is violating in any event by disregarding the United Nations charter).

Some countries want to bombard Syria in order to stop the atrocities or counter Iran or lift favored rebel groups to power. Other countries want Syria left alone. But no country (except perhaps France) sees any sense in a limited strike to punish Syria for using chemical weapons—and, moreover, in such a way as to sting but not topple Assad's government, a view shared by Sen. John McCain as well. You either kill the rattlesnake or leave it alone; you don't poke it with a stick. So Obama's international law theory failed not just because of its legal defects, but because it did not mesh with political realities. When Obama charged ahead nonetheless, he found himself naked and alone, and he turned to Congress for cover.

Periodical and Internet Sources Bibliography

The following articles have been selected to supplement the diverse views presented in this chapter.

Ben Armbruster	"Former Top CIA Official Says U.S. Should Not Help Syrian Rebels Topple Assad," *Talking Points Memo*, September 16, 2013. http://thinkprogress.org.
Henry Blodget	"Ambassador Samantha Power: This Is Why the US Must Attack Syria," *Business Insider*, September 9, 2013. www.businessinsider.com.
John Glaser	"Obama Waives Ban on Arming Terrorists So He Can Aid Syrian Rebels," *AntiWar.blog*, September 17, 2013. http://antiwar.com.
Robert E. Kelly	"Syria and the Capping of Executive War Powers," *The Diplomat*, October 7, 2013. http://thediplomat.com.
Jack Kenny	"Ex-Defense Chiefs Say Obama Can Strike Syria Without OK from Congress," *New American*, September 21, 2013.
Ezra Klein	"Obama's Proposed Syria Strikes Are 'Largely' Divorced from the Interests of the Syrian People," *Wonkblog*, September 2, 2013. www.washingtonpost.com.
Ernesto Londoño and Greg Miller	"U.S. Weapons Reaching Syrian Rebels," *Washington Post*, September 11, 2013.
Noel Sheppard	"WaPo's King: Congressional Defeat on Syria 'Would Diminish Obama's Presidency,'" *Newsbusters*, September 7, 2013. http://newsbusters.org.

OPPOSING
VIEWPOINTS®
SERIES

CHAPTER 2

What Is the Status of the Syrian Resistance?

Chapter Preface

Saudi Arabia has been one of the most ardent and consistent supporters of the Syrian resistance fighting against the government of Bashar al-Assad. The reasons for this support have been both strategic and religious. Iran, one of Saudi Arabia's main regional rivals, is a major ally of Assad's regime. So is Russia, a nation with which Saudi Arabia has a long history of conflict. The Saudis funded and helped organize the Islamic resistance to Russian rule of Afghanistan through the 1980s.

In addition to political opposition to Iran and Russia, Saudi Arabia wants to help the resistance in Syria for sectarian reasons. Iran and the militant Lebanese organization Hezbollah, which are fighting for Assad, are primarily Shiite Muslims, while Saudi Arabia is Sunni Muslim.

In some ways, Saudi involvement in Syria dovetails with American aims. The United States has called for Assad's removal and has provided some support to the rebels fighting against him. In a June 25, 2013, discussion on National Public Radio, foreign correspondent Deb Amos said that the Saudis have coordinated with the United States and initially agreed to American suggestions that only light arms should be provided to the rebels. However, Amos says, in summer 2013 the Saudis began to provide more advanced weaponry to the rebels, including antiaircraft missiles.

It seems like the United States should be happy to have the Saudis arm groups that have US support; however, the situation is complicated. Many rebel groups in Syria have ties to Islamic extremist groups. Saudi Arabia is much more comfortable with at least some of those groups than is the United States.

Counterterrorism analyst Jonathan Schanzer in a February 27, 2012, *Foreign Poicy* article points out that this situation has uncomfortable precedents. As already mentioned, Saudi Arabia supported the radical Islamic groups who fought against Soviet control of Afghanistan. The United States also supported the groups fighting against the Soviets. That resistance was successful in forcing the Russians out of Afghanistan, but it also radicalized and trained a generation of Islamic extremist fighters and terrorists, including Osama bin Laden, who was responsible for the 9/11 attacks on the United States. In Afghanistan, Schanzer concludes, "the Saudis didn't simply counter communism. They fueled a generation of zealous Islamist fighters who later caused bigger problems elsewhere." Schanzer worries that Saudi support of rebels in Syria may have similar effects. "The Iranians and Russians may yet pay a price for propping up Assad in Syria," he warns, adding that "if the Saudis have their way, the world may pay a price too."

The authors in this chapter debate whether the United States should arm the Syrian rebels, whether the rebels have used chemical weapons, and whether a rebel victory in Syria is desirable.

> *"The rivalry between the groups is a reminder of how divided Syria's rebel factions are."*

Moderate and Radical Groups Vie for Control of Resistance in Syria

David Enders

David Enders is a special correspondent for McClatchy news service. In the following viewpoint, he reports on the tension between Syrian rebel groups, some of which are moderate and some of which are radical. He says that there has been fighting between the two factions and notes that some Islamic groups are affiliated with the terrorist group al Qaeda. The secular faction expects that they will have to fight against the radical groups, either before or after Syrian president Bashar Assad is overthrown.

As you read, consider the following questions:

1. What is the Nusra Front, as described by Enders?

2. What is the Islamic State of Iraq, according to the author?

3. What does Enders say the Sahwa Movement was?

Two Syrian rebel groups—one seeking an elected civil government, the other favoring the establishment of a religious state—are battling each other in the city of Tal Abyad, on the border with Turkey, in a sign of the tensions that are likely to rule this country if the government of President Bashar Assad falls.

Four people were killed [in late March 2013] in fighting here between the Farouq Battalions, which favors elections, and Jabhat al Nusra, or the Nusra Front, which the United States has declared an al Qaida-affiliated terrorist group. Since then, Farouq has been massing men here in an example of the growing friction that's emerged in recent months as Nusra has captured strategic infrastructure across Syria's north and east, including oil and gas installations, grain silos and a hydroelectric dam.

Resistance-Controlled Areas of Syria

Raqqa province, where Tal Abyad is, and Hasaka province, to the east, are poverty-stricken but vital to Syria's agriculture. Hasaka and Deir el Zour province to the south are the center of the country's oil industry.

"They want to control the border crossing here," said Abu Mansour, a member of Farouq in Tal Abyad. Like other rebels, he uses a nom de guerre [French for "name of war"; that is, an alias] to hide his identity from the government.

The rivalry between the groups is a reminder of how divided Syria's rebel factions are and how inaccurate it is to refer to the anti-Assad forces as if they were a single group, with a single goal. Indeed, while news stories for months often referred to rebels as the Free Syrian Army, that term is more an idea than an organization. Instead, the rebel movement comprises dozens of groups whose ideologies have only one common goal: the toppling of the Assad regime.

Farouq, which has battalions across Syria and espouses a moderate interpretation of Islam, controls border crossings with Turkey at Tal Abyad and Bab al Hawa, in northwestern Syria. Nusra has attempted to seize control of both crossing points since Farouq took them from pro-Assad forces last September [2012].

The rivalry between the groups has become increasingly apparent as Nusra raises the volume of its calls for Islamic law. Recently, it suggested it might declare Raqqa, the largest city under rebel control, the center of an Islamic emirate. Last November, the group clashed with members of Kurdish militias after it seized the border crossing at Ras al Ayn.

Sunday's fighting badly wounded Mohammad al Daher, a popular Farouq leader known as Abu Azzam who'd also fought Nusra-affiliated militants at Bab al Hawa last year. He was taken to Turkey for treatment, and friends said he remained in intensive care Tuesday.

Sectarian Battles

In candid moments, members of Nusra don't deny their links to al Qaida in Iraq and the Islamic State of Iraq, the al Qaida-linked group that battled U.S. troops there and continues to carry out attacks. All three groups call for establishing Islamic states in the areas in which they operate, in Syria and Iraq, and view non-Sunni Muslims as apostates who've rejected Islamic teachings. That includes Alawites, the sect to which Assad and about 10 percent of Syrians belong, as well as Shiite Muslims, who make up the majority of Iraqis and have dominated the government there since the fall of dictator Saddam Hussein.

Nusra has taken tough action against those who oppose its fundamentalist beliefs. In the city of Shadadeh, in southern Hasaka province, members of a moderate rebel group said Nusra members had dispersed a demonstration against them earlier this month by firing heavy machine guns in the air. A

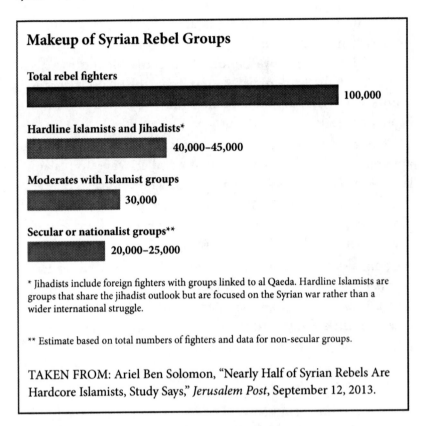

Makeup of Syrian Rebel Groups

Total rebel fighters

100,000

Hardline Islamists and Jihadists*

40,000–45,000

Moderates with Islamist groups

30,000

Secular or nationalist groups**

20,000–25,000

* Jihadists include foreign fighters with groups linked to al Qaeda. Hardline Islamists are groups that share the jihadist outlook but are focused on the Syrian war rather than a wider international struggle.

** Estimate based on total numbers of fighters and data for non-secular groups.

TAKEN FROM: Ariel Ben Solomon, "Nearly Half of Syrian Rebels Are Hardcore Islamists, Study Says," *Jerusalem Post*, September 12, 2013.

similar event occurred in the city of Mayadeen, in Deir el Zour province, after locals demonstrated against Nusra's establishment of an Islamic court there.

"They call us kufar," or non-Muslims, said Abu Mohammed, who leads a rebel brigade in Shadadeh. "We will have no choice but to be like the Sahwa," he said, referring to the tribal movement in Iraq that began in 2006 to kick al Qaida in Iraq followers from that country's western province of Anbar, which borders Hasaka and Deir el Zour. The Sahwa movement was crucial to American pacification efforts.

Members of other rebel groups increasingly liken Nusra to the Syrian government in its intolerance of any opposition, and they fear its spies. Nusra has detained secular activists who've spoken against it.

Abu Mansour said that for now, Nusra had withdrawn from Tal Abyad. But he expected more fighting.

"It seems we cannot deal with them peacefully," he said, "So it seems inevitable we will fight them, whether it is before the regime falls or after."

| "Nowhere in rebel-controlled Syria is there a secular fighting force to speak of."

Syrian Rebel Groups Dominated by Islamists

Ben Hubbard

Ben Hubbard is the Middle East correspondent for the New York Times. *In the following viewpoint, he reports that there is virtually no secular resistance group in Syria. Instead, he says, groups with radical views, including those affiliated with the terrorist organization al Qaeda, are the most influential and the most powerful. As the war has gone on, he says, opposition to Syrian president Bashar Assad has become increasingly radicalized, though there does remain a moderate Islamic resistance.*

As you read, consider the following questions:

1. What is the Supreme Military Council, and how has it failed to meet US expectations, in Hubbard's opinion?

2. According to the author, who formed the vanguard of the rebellion at the beginning?

3. What is the difference between the Nusra Front and Ahrar al-Sham, as described by Hubbard?

In Syria's largest city, Aleppo, rebels aligned with Al Qaeda control the power plant, run the bakeries, and head a court that applies Islamic law. Elsewhere, they have seized government oil fields, put employees back to work, and now profit from the crude they produce.

Across Syria, rebel-held areas are dotted with Islamic courts staffed by lawyers and clerics, and by fighting brigades led by extremists.

Even the Supreme Military Council, the umbrella rebel organization whose formation the West had hoped would sideline radical groups, is stocked with commanders who want to infuse Islamic law into a future Syrian government.

Nowhere in rebel-controlled Syria is there a secular fighting force to speak of.

This is the landscape President Obama confronts as he considers how to respond to growing evidence that Syrian officials have used chemical weapons, crossing a red line he had set. More than two years of violence has radicalized the armed opposition fighting the government of President Bashar Assad, leaving few groups with both a political vision the United States shares and the military might to push it forward.

Among the most extreme is the notorious Al Nusra Front, the Al Qaeda–aligned force declared a terrorist organization by the United States, but other groups also share aspects of its Islamist ideology in varying degrees.

"Some of the more extremist opposition is very scary from an American perspective and that presents us with all sorts of problems," said Ari Ratner, a fellow at the Truman National Security Project and former Middle East adviser for the Obama administration. "We have no illusions about the prospect of engaging with the Assad regime—it must still go—but we are also very reticent to support the more hard-line rebels."

Syrian officials recognize that the United States is worried that it has few natural allies in the armed opposition and have tried to exploit that with a public campaign to persuade, or frighten, Washington into staying out of the fight. At every turn they promote the notion that the alternative to Assad is an extremist Islamic state.

The Islamist character of the opposition reflects the main constituency of the rebellion, which has been led since its start by Syria's Sunni Muslim majority, mostly in conservative, marginalized areas.

The descent into brutal civil war has hardened sectarian differences and the failure of more mainstream rebel groups to secure regular arms supplies has allowed Islamists to fill the void and win supporters.

The religious agenda of the combatants sets them apart from many civilian activists, protesters, and aid workers who hoped the uprising would create a civil, democratic Syria.

When the armed rebellion began, defectors from the government's staunchly secular army formed the vanguard. The rebel movement has since grown to include fighters with a wide range of views, including Al Qaeda–aligned jihadis seeking to establish an Islamic emirate, political Islamists inspired by the Muslim Brotherhood, and others who want an Islamic-influenced legal code like that found in many Arab states.

"My sense is that there are no seculars," said Elizabeth O'Bagy of the Institute for the Study of War.

Of most concern to the United States is the Nusra Front, whose leader recently confirmed that the group cooperated with Al Qaeda in Iraq and pledged fealty to Al Qaeda's top leader, Ayman al-Zawahri, Osama bin Laden's longtime deputy. Nusra has claimed responsibility for a number of suicide bombings and is the group of choice for the foreign jihadis pouring into Syria.

Another prominent group, Ahrar al-Sham, shares much of Nusra's extremist ideology but is mostly made up of Syrians.

The two groups are most active in the north and east and are widely respected among other rebels for their fighting abilities and their ample arsenal, much of it given by sympathetic donors in the Gulf. And both helped lead campaigns to seize military bases, dams on the Euphrates River and the provincial capital of Raqqa province in March, the only regional capital entirely held by rebel forces.

In the oil-rich provinces of Deir al-Zour and Hasaka, Nusra fighters have seized government oil fields, putting some under the control of tribal militias and running others themselves. "They are the strongest military force in the area," said the commander of a Hasaka rebel brigade reached via Skype. "We can't deny it."

But most of its fighters joined the group for the weapons, he said, not the ideology, and that some left after discovering the Al Qaeda connection.

"Most of the youth who joined them did so to topple the regime, not because they wanted to join Al Qaeda," he said, speaking on the condition of anonymity.

As extremists rose in the rebel ranks, the United States sought to limit their influence, first by designating Nusra a terrorist organization, and later by pushing for the formation of a Supreme Military Council that is linked to the main exile opposition group, the Syrian National Coalition.

"There was undeniable evidence that chemical weapons had been used in a deadly attack against a rebel enclave."

"Little Doubt" Syria Gassed Opposition

Adam Entous, Dion Nissenbaum, and Maria Abi-Habib

Adam Entous, Dion Nissenbaum, and Maria Abi-Habib are journalists with the Wall Street Journal. *In the following viewpoint they report that the Barack Obama Administration is certain that Syrian president Bashar Assad's government used poison gas against its enemies, killing one thousand, including many civilians and children. The writers report that there is evidence that the gas was delivered with Syrian government rockets, and so did not come from Syrian rebel groups, as Assad has claimed. The writers say that Obama believes that an attack on Syria is necessary to show that the use of chemical weapons cannot be tolerated.*

As you read, consider the following questions:

1. What actions by Syria did Secretary of State John Kerry say indicated that Assad had something to hide, according to the authors?

2. What concrete military actions has the United States taken to ready for a possible attack on Syria, according to the authors?

3. According to Entous, Nissenbaum, and Abi-Habib, why does the United States not want Assad to lose control of his chemical weapons?

In harsh, uncompromising language, Secretary of State John Kerry began laying out the U.S. case for possible military action against Syria, saying there was undeniable evidence that chemical weapons had been used in a deadly attack against a rebel enclave and that it was "a moral obscenity."

Obama administration planning centers on carrying out any U.S. and allied strikes on Syria as part of a coalition without United Nations backing, U.S. and European officials said. Such a route could raise international law concerns but would let the administration avoid a potentially protracted diplomatic fight at the U.N. with Russia, President Bashar al-Assad's main backer on the Security Council. The U.S. has stepped up contacts with its North Atlantic Treaty Organization partners and the Arab League about supporting such an operation.

The U.S.'s stepped-up public rhetoric and war planning laid the groundwork for President Barack Obama to make a swift decision on launching airstrikes, even as administration officials made clear they are still awaiting the results of a final U.S. intelligence assessment on alleged chemical attacks last week that activists and rebels say killed more than 1,000 Syrians.

For now, senior administration officials said the U.S. has concluded there is "no doubt" chemical weapons were used in the incident. The administration said the evidence leaves "little doubt" that forces loyal to Mr. Assad were responsible for using the chemical weapons. U.S. intelligence agencies are now in the process of firming up those conclusions, officials said.

"The indiscriminate slaughter of civilians, the killing of women and children and innocent bystanders by chemical weapons is a moral obscenity," Mr. Kerry said in Washington, saying Damascus's delays in allowing international monitors to reach sites of last week's alleged attacks indicated it had something to hide, and saying that the U.S. and its allies are "actively consulting" on how to respond.

"President Obama believes there must be accountability for those who would use the world's most heinous weapons against the world's most vulnerable people," Mr. Kerry said.

His statement came after U.N. inspectors faced gunfire Monday from unidentified snipers as they investigated reports of a chemical-weapons attack last week in the Damascus suburb of Mouadhamiya, one of the areas allegedly struck last week in poison-gas attacks.

The U.S. had earlier delivered a caution to U.N. Secretary-General Ban Ki-moon, with a senior official telling him the inspection mission was pointless and no longer safe, said a person familiar with the matter. Mr. Ban ordered his team to continue their work, this person said.

The U.N. investigators are mandated to determine whether chemical attacks occurred, but not who initiated them. U.S. officials said Monday they expected their own intelligence assessment on the attacks, details of which could be released publicly as early as Tuesday, to conclude that forces loyal to Mr. Assad were behind the poison-gas attack, not the rebels, as the Assad regime and Russia have alleged.

Administration officials made clear Mr. Obama would make his decision based on the U.S. assessment and not the findings brought back by the U.N. inspectors.

The U.S. evidence includes an analysis by U.S. spy agencies of the type of rocket used in last week's assaults to deliver chemical weapons. The agencies concluded that the type of rocket used was solely in the possession of regime forces, not

UN Inspectors on Chemical Weapons Use in Syria

On the basis of the evidence obtained during our investigation of the Ghouta incident, the conclusion is that, on 21 August 2013, chemical weapons have been used in the ongoing conflict between the parties in the Syrian Arab Republic, also against civilians, including children, on a relatively large scale.

In particular, the environmental, chemical and medical samples we have collected provide clear and convincing evidence that surface-to-surface rockets containing the nerve agent Sarin were used in Ein Tarma, Moadamiyah and Zamalka in the Ghouta area of Damascus.

United Nations Report on the Alleged Use of Chemical Weapons in the Ghouta Area of Damascus on 21 August 2013.

the opposition, providing the White House with greater certainty of Mr. Assad's involvement, according to U.S. officials.

Pentagon officials said potential regime targets have been identified and commanders are awaiting a green light from Mr. Obama, underlining the speed with which the U.S. could act against Mr. Assad.

The U.S. Navy's Sixth Fleet has four warships in the eastern Mediterranean awaiting orders, Navy officials said. They are equipped with Tomahawk missiles and other weapon systems that can reach across Syria.

Options under consideration by the White House call for using long-range cruise missiles to take out Syrian military and intelligence command and control sites and other regime targets, U.S. officials said.

The goal of such strikes, a senior defense official said, would be to "deter and degrade" Mr. Assad's regime by raising the price for chemical weapons use and making it harder for his forces to deploy them in the future.

The U.S. warships are being kept a "healthy distance from the coast" as a precaution against Mr. Assad's advanced Russian-made coastal defenses, which include recently upgraded Yakhont missiles, a senior defense official said. U.S. officials discount the possibility that Mr. Assad might try to target U.S. warships because they are out of reach and because doing so could trigger a more devastating American response.

Administration and defense officials described the potential strikes as limited in scope, saying the goal would be to send a message to Mr. Assad without attempting to remove him.

Approval for strikes from NATO, should the U.S. seek formal backing, would require a member consensus.

There are a range of reasons for a limited response. The administration has little appetite for a protracted fight, so it is drawing a distinction between strikes aimed at the use of chemical weapons and other efforts to strengthen the Syrian opposition.

In addition, the U.S. doesn't want Mr. Assad to lose control of the chemical weapons because of the danger that they could fall into the hands of extremists. Moreover, the fall of Mr. Assad could give al Qaeda greater sway over large tracts of the country, say officials who favor only limited strikes to punish him for chemical weapons use.

For more than two years, Mr. Obama avoided U.S. military involvement in Syria's civil war. But his position has hardened considerably in response to last week's incident.

A major concern for Mr. Obama is whether U.S. inaction could embolden Mr. Assad to use chemical weapons again on a wide scale, despite Mr. Obama's declaration last year that doing so would cross his "red line."

From a strategic standpoint, advocates of limited strikes on government targets say such action is needed to burnish the Obama administration's credibility should it threaten to use military action in the future.

"He absolutely needs to act," said Aaron David Miller, a former Middle East negotiator at the State Department now at the Woodrow Wilson International Center for Scholars. "Now everyone says 'no' to the United States without cost or consequence."

Others said that Mr. Obama needs to go beyond cruise-missile strikes. "Simply taking reprisal action to say 'We mean it' does not strike me as significant meaningful action," said Anthony Cordesman, a longtime military analyst at the Center for Strategic and International Studies. "It's a pointless punitive military exercise."

White House spokesman Jay Carney made clear that the question wasn't whether Mr. Obama would respond, but how and when. "The president and his team believes that there needs to be a response that reflects the seriousness of this transgression," he said.

Once he has made that decision, he will address the American people, Mr. Carney said. The White House also began contacting lawmakers, part of a consultative process sought by members of Congress.

Late Tuesday, the State Department postponed talks with Russia that had been scheduled for later this week on a proposed peace conference on Syria, reflecting the administration's focus on the chemical weapons incident.

In addition to the rockets, officials said tissue samples extracted from the attack scenes and analyzed by the U.S. and its allies provide evidence that chemical weapons were used.

In addition to its assessment that the Assad regime is the only entity in Syria capable of carrying out such a large-scale attack, the official said, the U.S. is also tracking the regime's chemical-weapons stockpiles. That effort has provided evidence connecting the regime to this attack, the official said.

The U.N. confirmed that its investigators had come under fire Monday morning as they set out to investigate reports of a chemical-weapons attack last week in Mouadhamiya. The U.N. team turned back. Later in the day, they made it to two hospitals, interviewed survivors and doctors, and collected samples, Mr. Ban said in a statement.

In activist videos posted Monday, U.N. investigators could be seen at one field hospital wearing their signature bright blue helmets and bulletproof vests, hovering above patients being treated for exposure to the suspected chemical weapons.

"What was your location?" one U.N. inspector asked a gaunt-looking male patient seemingly in his 40s.

"I was in Al Rawda mosque," the man replied.

"What did you feel?" the inspector probed.

"It was [about] a minute and then I passed out," the patient replied, to which the translator added he had "convulsions upon his arrival."

The American message to Mr. Ban was that the U.S. believed there wasn't adequate security for the U.N. inspectors to visit the affected areas to conduct their mission, a senior administration official said. The administration also told the U.N. that the U.S. didn't think the inspectors would be able to collect viable evidence owing to the passage of time and damage from subsequent shelling, this person said. The U.N. has said such evidence would still exist.

Western governments joined Mr. Kerry in taking an increasingly stern line against Damascus.

"The suspected large-scale use of poison gas breaks a taboo even in this Syrian conflict that has been so full of cruelty," Chancellor Angela Merkel's spokesman, Steffen Seibert, said Monday. "It's a serious breach of the international Chemical Weapons Convention, which categorically bans the use of these weapons. It must be punished; it cannot remain without consequences."

The U.K. said it is "clear" that the Assad regime was behind last week's attack. British Prime Minister David Cameron cut short his holiday in order to return to London for a U.K. National Security Council meeting that has been called for Wednesday.

"Evidence from casualties and medical staff indicated that rebel forces in the [Syrian] civil war had used the deadly nerve agent sarin".

UN Accuses Syrian Rebels of Carrying Out Sarin Gas Attacks Which Had Been Blamed on Assad's Troops

Damien Gayle

Damien Gayle is a reporter for London's Daily Mail *newspaper. In the following viewpoint, he reports that a United Nations official and investigator believes that Syrian rebels may have used the nerve gas sarin against Syrian government forces. This contradicts claims by the United States that it was Assad's regime that used poison gas against the rebels and civilians. Gayle notes that the UN itself has been reluctant to make a definitive statement regarding which side has or has not used chemical weapons, concluding that there is not yet sufficient evidence to determine who is responsible.*

As you read, consider the following questions:

1. Who does Gayle say that Carla Del Ponte has interviewed in her investigations?

2. Why did Israel say it had carried out air strikes on Syria, according to the author?

3. How does sarin gas cause damage, as described by Gayle?

A senior United Nations official has claimed that Syrian rebels may have used chemical weapons against government forces.

Carla Del Ponte said evidence from casualties and medical staff indicated that rebel forces in the civil war had used the deadly nerve agent sarin.

'Our investigators have been in neighbouring countries interviewing victims, doctors and field hospitals, and there are strong, concrete suspicions, but not yet incontrovertible proof, of the use of sarin gas,' said Del Ponte in an interview with Swiss-Italian television.

'This was use on the part of the opposition, the rebels, not by the government authorities.'

Last night, the UN commission looking into allegations of war crimes in Syria tried to row back on the comments by its human rights investigator, pointing out that conclusive evidence had not been discovered.

However, the White House said it was likely that President Bashar al-Assad's regime, not the rebels, were behind any chemical weapons use.

Syrian government forces and the rebels have already accused each other of carrying out three attacks with chemical weapons.

Sarin has been classed as a weapon of mass destruction due to its potency and is banned under international law.

US President Barack Obama has said that the use or deployment of chemical weapons in Syria would cross a 'red line' that could lead to foreign military intervention.

Following two Israeli air strikes on military bases in the Syrian capital of Damascus over the weekend, a Russian foreign ministry spokesman said: 'We are seriously concerned by the signs of preparation for possible armed intervention in Syria.'

As a long-standing Syrian ally, Russia has protected President Assad by blocking Western efforts in the UN Security Council to push him from power. Israeli officials claim the air strikes were to ensure Lebanon's Hezbollah did not receive a shipment of hi-tech missiles that could threaten Israel.

The comments by Ms Del Ponte, a member of the U.N. panel probing alleged war crimes in Syria, contradict claims by Britain and the U.S. that intelligence reports showed Syrian soldiers had used chemical weapons.

She said that the United Nations independent commission of inquiry on Syria has not yet seen evidence of government forces having used chemical weapons, which are banned under international law.

'Our investigators have been in neighbouring countries interviewing victims, doctors and field hospitals and, according to their report of last week which I have seen, there are strong, concrete suspicions but not yet incontrovertible proof of the use of sarin gas, from the way the victims were treated,' said Ms Del Ponte.

The odourless, colourless nerve agent prevents the proper operation of the enzyme acetylcholinesterase, the nervous system's 'off switch' for glands and muscles.

Without this enzyme muscles are continually stimulated leading to convulsions, paralysis, unconsciousness and eventually respiratory failure leading to death.

The History of Sarin Gas

The use of chemical weapons was banned by the Geneva Protocol (agreement) in 1925. But scientists continued to experiment with new and deadlier chemical compounds.

In 1936 German scientist Gerhard Schrader was doing research on insecticides when he came up with a terrible substance. It was so toxic, Schrader found he couldn't even work with it. He called it tabun.

Tabun is a nerve gas. When it is inhaled or absorbed through the skin, it attacks a victim's nervous system (the brain, spinal cord, and network of nerves that control the muscles). If the victim is exposed to enough tabun, every muscle in the body begins to contract. The victim vomits, goes into convulsions, and suffocates to death.

The German army quickly learned of Schrader's discovery. After watching a demonstration of the gas, they ordered tabun into production. Schrader, however, wasn't finished yet. In 1938 he discovered a compound that turned out to be ten times as poisonous as tabun. He named it sarin. A year later, scientists in Berlin, Germany, produced the first batch of Sarin Gas.

Judith Herbst,
The History of Weapons, 2006.

Ms Del Ponte, a former Swiss attorney-general who also served as prosecutor of the International Criminal Tribunal for the former Yugoslavia, gave no details as to when or where sarin may have been used.

Assad's government and the rebels accuse another of carrying out three chemical weapon attacks, one near Aleppo and another near Damascus, both in March, and another in Homs in December.

Meanwhile fighting continued to rage in Syria, where rebels claimed to have killed eight government troops after shooting down their helicopter in the eastern province of Deir el-Zour, along Syria's border with Iraq.

The Coventry-based Syrian Observatory for Human Rights posted footage online showing several armed men standing in front of the wreckage.

As one of the fighters in the video speaks, the camera pans to a pick-up truck piled with bodies. The fighter is then heard saying that all of Assad's troops who were on board the helicopter were killed as it crashed.

He says Islamic fighters of the Abu Bakr Saddiq brigade brought down the helicopter as it was taking off from a nearby air base in the provincial capital.

The Observatory, which claims to get its information via a network of activists on the ground, said eight troops were killed in the incident.

Rebels also yesterday occupied parts of the Mannagh military air base after weeks of fighting with government troops who have for months been defending the sprawling facility near the border with Turkey.

Assad's warplanes were pounding rebel positions inside the base today as battles between rebels and government forces raged on, the Observatory said, adding there was an unknown number of casualties on both sides.

The rebels moved deep into the air base yesterday despite fire from government warplanes, capturing a tank unit inside and killing the base commander, claimed the Aleppo Media Centre, another activist group.

The fighting comes a day after Israeli warplanes struck areas in and around the capital, Damascus, setting off a series of explosions as they targeted a shipment of guided missiles believed to be bound for Hezbollah.

The airstrike, the second in three days and the third this year, signalled a sharp escalation of Israel's involvement in Syria's civil war.

Syrian state media reported that Israeli missiles hit a military and scientific research centre near Damascus and caused casualties. The reports did not specify the number or say if the casualties were civilians or troops.

The state-run Sana news agency made no mention of the fighting inside the Mannagh air base. But it reported that government troops today regained control of villages along the highway linking the northern city of Aleppo to its civilian airport, the country's second largest.

Syrian 'armed forces restored security and stability to (six) villages' south of the city and along the airport highway, Sana said, calling it a 'major strategic victory in the north'.

Much of the north has been in opposition hands since rebels launched an offensive in the area last summer, seizing army bases, large swathes of land along the border with Turkey and whole neighbourhoods inside Aleppo.

The Syrian conflict started in 2011 with protests against Assad's regime, but eventually turned into a civil war that according to UN estimates has so far killed more than 70,000 people.

More than one million Syrians have fled their homes during the fighting and sought shelter in neighbouring countries such as Jordan, Lebanon and Turkey. Millions of others have been displaced inside the country.

"America has changed its mind and has backed away from . . . all these Islamic [rebel] groups. . . . Advantage, Assad."

Assad Will Defeat the Rebels

Michael Hirsh

Michael Hirsh is chief correspondent for the National Journal. *In the following viewpoint, he argues that the Barack Obama Administration has realized that supporting radical Islamic rebels in Syria will be detrimental to US interests. As evidence, Hirsh points to Egypt, where the United States did not intervene to help the less radical Muslim Brotherhood against the Egyptian regime. Hirsh concludes that Assad will not be driven from power, and that the Arab Spring, in which dictatorial regimes across the Middle East faced protests and revolution, is over.*

As you read, consider the following questions:

1. According to Hirsh, what matters more than the accusation of chemical-weapon use by Assad?

2. How did the Arab Spring begin, in the US interpretation, according to Hirsh?

3. What does the author say is Obama's biggest problem in terms of credibility?

Bashar al-Assad is, finally, having a very good week [in late August 2013].

The latest allegations of chemical-weapons use against the Syrian dictator don't matter nearly as much as other dramatic developments—in particular, the United States' willingness to stand aside while Assad's autocratic brethren in the Egyptian junta cold-bloodedly killed some one thousand protesters, supported by the Saudis and Gulf states.

The End of the Arab Spring

And this week, the chairman of the Joint Chiefs of Staff, Gen. Martin Dempsey, finally said plainly what Obama administration officials have been thinking privately since June, the last time Washington said its "red line" had been crossed and pledged military aid to the Syrian rebels—then did nothing. In a letter to Rep. Eliot Engel, D-N.Y., Dempsey said flatly that U.S. aid to the rebels now would just end up arming radical, possibly al-Qaida-linked groups. And Obama wasn't going to allow that to happen.

What it all means is that we may now be at a historic turning point in the Arab Spring[1]—what is effectively the end of it, at least for now. Assad, says Syria expert Joshua Landis, is surely taking on board the lessons of the last few weeks: If the United States wasn't going to intervene or even protest very loudly over the killing of mildly radical Muslim Brotherhood supporters, it's certainly not going to take a firmer hand against Assad's slaughter of even more radical anti-U.S. groups. "With a thousand people dead or close to it, and America still debating whether to cut off aid, and how and when, that's got to give comfort to Assad," says Landis, a professor at the University of Oklahoma. "The Egyptians brushed off the United States and said. . . . Well, we don't want to end up like Syria.

---

1. The Arab Spring was a wave of demonstrations and revolutions in Arab nations that began in December 2010.

And America blinked. And Israel and the Gulf states were in there telling them to hit the protesters hard."

What began, in the U.S. interpretation, as an inspiring drive for democracy and freedom from dictators and public corruption has now become, for Washington, a coldly realpolitik calculation. As the Obama administration sees it, the military in Egypt is doing the dirty work of confronting radical political Islam, if harshly. In Syria, the main antagonists are both declared enemies of the United States, with Bashar al-Assad and Iran-supported Hezbollah aligning against al-Qaida-linked Islamist militias. Why shouldn't Washington's policy be to allow them to engage each other, thinning the ranks of each?

And by all accounts, the administration and the Pentagon simply don't want to risk the "blowback" that could occur if the Assad regime collapses and serious weapons fall into the hands of al-Qaida. As one Washington-based military expert points out, Assad is just not enough of a threat to U.S. interests. "Look at how long it took us to decide to back the [Afghani] mujahedeen in the 1980s against the Soviet Union. Syria is not the Soviet Union," the expert says.

Democracy Is Not the Issue

Dempsey, in his letter, said that deciding what to do about Syria "is not about choosing between two sides but rather about choosing one among many sides." He added that "the side we choose must be ready to promote their interests and ours when the balance shifts in their favor. Today, they are not."

On Wednesday, in a replay of what happened a year ago, the administration appeared to push for more time in ascertaining whether Assad had used chemical weapons. White House spokesman Josh Earnest said the administration was "deeply concerned by reports that hundreds of Syrian civilians have been killed in an attack by Syrian government

© Harley Schwadron/www.Cartoonstock.com.

forces, including by the use of chemical weapons," but was working "to gather additional information."

This is familiar ground. Back in June, Deputy National Security Adviser Ben Rhodes said in a statement that the administration would start supplying the Syrian rebels' "Supreme Military Council" and "consulting with Congress on these matters in the coming weeks." But there is little evidence that any military aid has reached the rebels.

President Obama's biggest problem in terms of his credibility is that he's wedded to a "narrative" that won't stand up to scrutiny any longer, says Landis. "We started this off saying it was about democracy and freedom. We've stuck to that interpretation. We didn't say this is about economic mismanagement and poverty," which is what the protests were largely about. But now "nobody believes they're democrats anymore. That's the problem. What we saw in Egypt signals that America has changed its mind and has backed away from the Muslim

Brotherhood and all these Islamic groups. And the Syrian rebel groups are to the right of the Muslim Brotherhood."

Advantage, Assad.

"The talk now is of the rebels driving [Assad] out of power by winning the war."

The Rebels Seem Poised to Defeat Assad

Bradley Klapper

Bradley Klapper covers US foreign policy for the Associated Press. In the following viewpoint he reports in 2012 on the success of the Syrian rebels. He notes that the rebels were making greater gains than the Barack Obama administration had anticipated, leading to the hope that they might overthrow Assad without American aid. Important defections from Assad's government also raised the possibility of a relatively quick end to the fighting, with Assad deposed.

As you read, consider the following questions:

1. What provisions were made in Kofi Annan's plan for a transitional Syrian government, according to the author?

2. According to Klapper, what is the goal of the US plan for a "soft landing" if Syria's government changes?

3. In what areas of Syria does Klapper say the rebels have managed to retain control?

With Syrian diplomacy all but dead, the Obama administration is shifting its focus on the civil war away from political transition and toward helping the rebels defeat the Syrian regime on the battlefield.

The US still wants to avoid any military involvement, banking on a complicated policy of indirect assistance to the rebels and hope that the ragtag alliance of militias can demoralize President Bashar Assad's better-armed forces and end the war without far greater casualties.

It's a scenario analysts see as unlikely, even as the opposition gains ground in Aleppo, Damascus and elsewhere, and as the cadre of high-level defections from Assad's government grows. Prime Minister Riad Hijab became the latest to abandon Assad on Monday, rebels said.

The defections are "the latest indication that Assad has lost control of Syria and that the momentum is with the opposition forces and the Syrian people," White House spokesman Tommy Vietor said.

"The regime is crumbling," State Department spokesman Patrick Ventrell said.

In Aleppo, the rebels are exceeding the expectations of military experts. Despite intense bombardment from warplanes, they've now withstood two weeks of regime counterattacks and are clawing toward the city center. Militiamen also are stepping up guerrilla-like forays in central districts of Damascus once firmly in Assad's hands.

Those gains have given the Obama administration hope that the tide of the war is turning—and without the need for the US to reconsider its opposition to airstrikes, no-fly zones or even weapons sales to the anti-Assad forces.

And with UN special envoy Kofi Annan quitting his diplomatic efforts and the rebels starting to carve out larger toeholds in Syrian territory, the US focus has changed accordingly.

Whereas once the US hoped to see a cease-fire to end the fighting and then Assad leave office eventually on his own, the talk now is of the rebels driving him out of power by winning the war—or of Assad's loyalists, in the face of more military setbacks, turning on their leader.

As the rebels gain ground and weaponry, the US has increased its humanitarian aid to $74 million and its "nonlethal" communications assistance to $25 million. The administration has eased restrictions for rebel fundraising in the United States.

It also has softened its support for the transitional plan crafted by Annan, and agreed to by both the United States and Russia after a conference in Geneva in June [2012]. The document aimed at establishing an interim government of individuals chosen by both the Assad regime and the opposition. Each would be able to veto candidates.

Contemplating Transition

The arrangement was rejected immediately by many in the Syrian opposition, and Ventrell relegated it on Monday [in early August 2012] to a "basis for a good framework." He said the transitional authority should be chosen by the opposition and "remnants of the regime that don't have blood on their hands"—cutting out Assad and his senior government officials.

"The future of Syria is going to be for the Syrians to decide," he said.

Speaking last week, Ventrell said: "We are not at a point where we are negotiating with the Assad regime. We are at a point where the opposition is gaining ground and making plans for the day after."

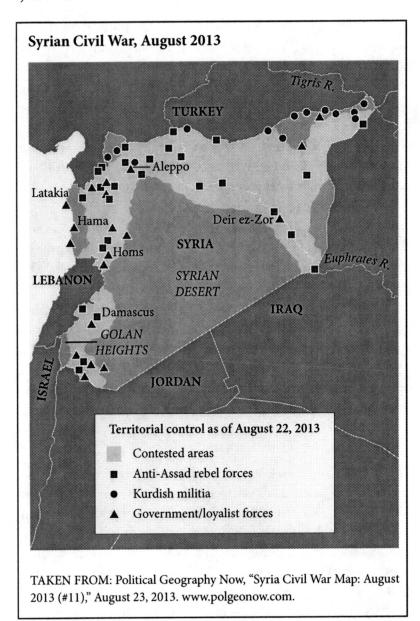

Syrian Civil War, August 2013

Territorial control as of August 22, 2013

- Contested areas
- ■ Anti-Assad rebel forces
- ● Kurdish militia
- ▲ Government/loyalist forces

TAKEN FROM: Political Geography Now, "Syria Civil War Map: August 2013 (#11)," August 23, 2013. www.polgeonow.com.

The statements follow more than a year of Obama administration officials speaking of bringing international diplomatic pressure to drive Assad from office and meeting with multinational groups like the Friends of Syria.

While officials maintain that they'd prefer a "peaceful political transition" take place, they concede privately that the deaths of at least 19,000 Syrians over the past 17 months, the utter refusal by Assad to compromise and the failure of diplomacy means more bloodshed may lie ahead.

With mediation efforts cut off, a rebel victory now appears among the most feasible path forward for an end to Syria's war. And US officials are trying to plan for messier regime change scenarios than the six-point plan advocated by Annan and adopted by no one in Syria.

The US ambassador to Syria, Robert Ford, held meetings with opposition leaders in Cairo [Egypt] last week. Those followed consultations that the State Department's Syria envoy, Fred Hof, held with activists and likeminded governments in Europe a week before. Secretary of State Hillary Rodham Clinton will talk to Syrian activists and Turkish officials in Istanbul this weekend, rejecting proposals to turn her visit into another international diplomatic forum.

Ventrell said the goal of much of the recent diplomacy was to help the opposition come up with a post-Assad plan that would be as cohesive as possible.

"There still has to be water, electricity and all the basic services," Ventrell said. "What will the government look like? How it will function the day after? How will we ensure that (Syria) doesn't descend into further sectarian chaos? How do we make it work? That's some of the things we're working on."

The approach is one that American officials liken to a "soft landing." The goal would be to avoid the power vacuum of post-Saddam Hussein's Iraq by salvaging as many elements of the state as possible, and avoiding new insurgencies from emerging.

"We want to get there in a way that's a softer landing," a US official said on condition of anonymity because he wasn't authorized to speak publicly on the matter. "We don't want to see the institutions just melt away."

Victory Still Uncertain

But it's unclear how quick the post-Assad era might come— and at what cost.

Most assessments see Syria's Assad making his stand in Damascus and battling to the end to hold his capital. Others speculate that regime loyalists could retreat to Alawite strongholds in northwest Syria, taking with them their guns, tanks, helicopters and even chemical weapons. Either situation could be extremely bloody. While Assad's forces are stretched, his Republican Guard units backed by airpower remain formidable.

And even as Clinton and other officials speak of the inevitability of opposition "safe zones" in Syria, the rebels have had to retreat from every major city they've held so far. They've maintained control of some rural areas bordering Turkey in the north, Lebanon in the west and Jordan in the south, according to the American Syrian Coalition.

The effect of the defections could be limited, as well. Like most previous regime members, those who fled Monday to Jordan were majority Sunnis. Assad still has the backing of the minority Alawite clan who hold most senior regime positions.

"It's politically important, but removing Assad and weakening his regime involves a political and military approach," said Andrew Tabler, a Syria expert at the Washington Institute for Near East Policy. "And it's the relative success of the military approach to date that has caused this defection."

> "In conceptualizing the horrific possibilities of a regime victory, we more clearly understand what's at stake in the Syria conflict."

An Assad Victory Would Be a Disaster

Brian Braun

Brian Braun works for the Atlantic Council, a Washington, DC–based think tank focused on Middle East policy. In the following viewpoint, he argues that President Bashar Assad's forces seem increasingly likely to achieve victory in Syria. He says that this will be a disaster in that it will exacerbate the refugee crisis, empower US enemies Iran and Hezbollah, and lead to genocidal atrocities. Braun suggests that the US current refusal to provide military aid to the rebels will not prevent an Assad victory and is not a helpful policy.

As you read, consider the following questions:

1. According to Braun, what has been the effect of the Syrian refugee crisis in Jordan?

2. What does the author say that Iran has done to help Assad's regime?

3. What cities will erupt in bloodshed if Assad wins, according to Braun?

The defeat of Syrian rebels in the strategic city of Qusair last week [June 2013] laid bare the impermanence of the opposition's slow-but-sure creep to victory against government forces loyal to Bashar Al-Assad. Supposedly inevitable, the prospect of rebel fighters ultimately overtaking the Syrian army on the battlefield is now in doubt, and intervention by the international community to save the struggling revolution becomes an even greater imperative as capable but unwilling powers like the United States continue to pursue a troubled diplomatic solution to the conflict.

A Catastrophic Victory Is Possible

Qusair may be but one in a string of regime victories in the weeks and months ahead that leads to the opposition's defeat. Imagine Assad's army does succeed in beating back the rebels. In this scenario, government forces reverse the hard-fought rebel gains in much of the north and east of the country and in greater Damascus—where the opposition is firmly rooted— and brutally reasserts government control over formerly liberated Syrian towns and villages. With the defeat of the so-called "terrorists", Assad emerges from the crisis with an incontestable grip on power and secures the survival of his autocratic regime.

Although the potential for a total regime victory remains remote, the consequences of a protracted or stalemated war are still very real and dangerous. Imagining such a scenario should compel the international community, and the United States in particular, to reassess the serious risks of failing to assist the opposition in overthrowing Assad. In conceptualizing the horrific possibilities of a regime victory, we more clearly understand what's at stake in the Syria conflict, and especially why intervening to halt Assad's army and strengthen the opposition is necessary to bring the conflict to an immediate end. What will an Assad victory lead to?

The Refugee Crisis

1. The refugee crisis will collapse the already-fragile regional humanitarian response. In response to Syria's refugee crisis, the UN last week asked for a record-breaking $5.1 billion in humanitarian aid. But that pales in comparison to what will be required if Assad wins. Even now the more than 1.6 million Syrian refugees living in Turkey, Jordan, Lebanon, and Iraq are dangerously straining the economies and threatening the stability of host countries. In Jordan, where crushing budget deficits and the reduction of subsidies have led to widespread discontent and violent clashes with the government, the millions required to feed, shelter, and treat the nearly 500,000 Syrian refugees in camps there now are already exploding the country's budget. In Lebanon and Turkey, which host more than 500,000 and 400,000 Syrian refugees, respectively, the inundation of refugees has outpaced the arrival of aid. Syrian families are moving into half-constructed houses and living under tents where they are vulnerable to disease and stretching already inadequate medical supplies. Estimates by the UN's Syria Regional Refugee Response anticipate the number of Syrian refugees abroad will increase to 3.5 million, and the number of internally displaced individuals will soar to a whopping 7 million by year's end. But these numbers are under current circumstances. Should Assad's army recapture opposition-held territory and unleash a mass wave of violence in stable, rebel-controlled areas, the figure would likely rise dramatically higher.

Enemies Empowered

2. Iran and [the militant Islamic Lebanese organization] Hezbollah will be empowered. Assad's regime is Iran's most

Alawites

The Alawites are an offshoot of the Shiite branch of Islam. It is believed the sect was founded on the Arabian Peninsula in the 9th century by a preacher named Mohammed ibn Nusayr. Their basic belief is that there is one God with a hierarchy of divine beings, the highest of whom is Ali ... hence the name Alawites, or "followers of Ali". . . .

Alawites have always suffered persecution at the hands of ruling Sunni dynasties. Saladin (Salah ad-Din) and his Ayyubid dynasty, the Mamluks and the Ottoman Turks massacred Alawite communities, forced them to convert or imposed crippling taxes. Alawites traditionally worked the poorest lands or held down the least skilled jobs. That situation radically changed early in the 20th century when the French courted the Alawites as allies and granted them a self-ruled enclave in the mountains around Lattakia. From there the Alawites entrenched themselves in Syrian national politics—with Hafez al-Assad, an Alawite, taking power in 1970.

Terry Carter, Les Dunston and Amelia Thomas,
Syria and Lebanon, 2008.

important ally and a vital partner against Israel. Losing Assad is not an option for Tehran [Iran], which has sent billions of dollars in economic and military assistance to sustain the Syrian regime since the conflict began despite Iran's own precarious economic situation. Succeeding in Syria would stave off complete regional isolation and strengthen its lifeline to its other regional ally Hezbollah. Hassan Nasrallah, Hezbollah's leader, is similarly so fearful of Assad's defeat that he sent militants to fight alongside regime forces in Syria, playing a decisive role in the victory at Qusair. Given the stunning rebel defeat there, Hezbollah is expected to send even more fighters to Syria. Hezbollah has also deployed a contingent to Aleppo where Assad's army is planning an assault to retake the city. Advances by Assad's army would also scatter rebel fighters to Syria's borders and spawn more deadly conflict across the region. Twin bombings linked to Assad's forces in the border city of Reyhanli, Turkey in May killed 51 people and injured 140 and are sure to be the first of many violent cross-border exchanges. Skirmishes in northern Lebanon have unsettled that country's delicate sectarian balance and threaten to cause devastating violence there as well. And in Iraq, where Al-Qaeda weapons and money are flowing unchecked between Syria's radical Al-Nusra Front and the anti-Maliki [hostile to Iraqi leader Nourial-Maliki] opposition, the backlash is inflaming an already tense sectarian situation that risks the very durability of Iraq's weak government.

3. Assad regime forces will exact revenge against the Sunni-majority opposition and perpetrate mass sectarian atrocities. As Assad's army retakes parts of the country held by the opposition, regime forces commanded by Assad's Alawite minority sect will carry out summary executions, imprisonment, and torture among the Sunni-majority opposition. In a country where the confessional [sectarian] balance has always been at risk of tipping, confessionally mixed cities like Horns and Damascus, where Alawites and Sunnis live in close proximity to one another, will erupt in sectarian bloodletting. Already reports have indicated that Assad's army has forcibly removed Sunni communities near Alawite areas to create protective buffer zones against attack. Atrocities will not be confined to Sunnis alone, however. Alawites and other minorities will be targeted by opposition forces in the panicked and chaotic rebel retreat and result in sectarian cleansing. In a recent report commissioned by the Center for the Prevention of Genocide at the U.S. Holocaust Memorial Museum, former ambas-

sador and Syria expert Frederic Hof warned that there is a high potential for genocidal acts as the conflict drags on, and cautioned that even a stalemated conflict would likely displace confessional communities to safer, more homogenous areas, heightening the risk of sectarian disintegration.

The U.S.'s current approach looks something like this: Decry Assad's abuses and hope that non-lethal assistance will be enough to sustain the opposition's gains. But as Qusair has shown, that approach is flawed and won't produce what we want to achieve in Syria: the replacement of Assad's regime with a stable and friendly new government. In reality, an Assad victory is just as likely as the stalemate that is developing now between the regime and opposition, and sadly the benefit of the doubt is not in our favor.

"An outright opposition victory would likely produce a momentary air of euphoria before the steep decline toward autocracy and darkness begin."

Don't Let the Syrian Rebels Win

Glenn E. Robinson

Glenn E. Robinson is associate professor at the Naval Postgraduate School. In the following viewpoint, he argues that the Syrian Muslim Brotherhood, which is a powerful force within the rebels, is extremely radical and dangerous. He also says that the Alawites, the Muslim minority denomination that holds power in Syria, faces serious danger if the regime of President Bashar al-Assad is defeated. He concludes that a negotiated settlement to the war is the best hope in Syria, as an outright rebel victory would result in violence and repression.

As you read, consider the following questions:

1. According to Robinson, why do the Alawites have few defenders in the Arab world?

2. Why is the Syrian Muslim Brotherhood different from its neighbors in Egypt, Tunisia, Jordan, and Morocco, according to the author?

3. Where does Robinson say that fighters battling the Syrian regime honed their skills?

It may well be true, as recent news reports tell us, that Bashar al-Assad's regime in Damascus, increasingly desperate in the face of an unrelenting rebel onslaught, is prepared to use chemical weapons against its own citizens. The Syrian leader himself, all the main power brokers in his government, and virtually all of the country's military officer corps come from a long-persecuted minority that legitimately fears that this war is a matter of "kill or be killed" for the Alawites, who make up around 12 percent of Syria's population. The Alawites left what is now Iraq a millennium ago and settled in the dusty hills of northwest Syria overlooking the Mediterranean. A doubly heretical sect in the eyes of orthodox Sunni Muslims—as an offshoot of Shiite Islam—the Alawites lived an isolated existence for centuries as their religion evolved to reflect various folk traditions.

The Alawites have few defenders in the Arab world, both because of the unorthodox nature of their religion and because of the horrible nature of the Baathist regime they have controlled since the 1960s. Nor does it help that they are widely seen as pawns of Iranian interests in the region. The regime's fall—which is still far from certain—will not be widely mourned in the Arab world, outside of Tehran and in Hezbollah circles.

The fall of the House of Assad will likely be celebrated by many in the West. But banking on the well-heeled Syrian expatriate community to come to power for any length of time is a losing bet. The exiles may have won the support of the Obama administration and others, but have little chance of holding power in Syria for any length of time, barring international occupation of the country. And nobody thinks the United States has any appetite to occupy another Arab country militarily, even for a relatively short period of time.

In other words, forget about the expats. The people that will ultimately take power in Syria are the armed men who control the country's streets, villages, and towns right now. They do not speak with a single voice, and are often people just looking to protect their families and communities from the Assads' onslaught. As for the rebel "Free Syrian Army," it is no army at all in the sense of having any kind of command and control over its constituent units.

What about the budding terrorist groups we hear so often about? The specter of foreign jihadis—al Qaeda and its fellow travellers—infiltrating the Syrian opposition and coming to power in Damascus is a silly, unrealistic notion promoted by those overeager to send in the U.S. Marines to Latakia. There is little evidence that foreign jihadis represent anything more than a sliver of those fighting the Assad regime.

But Syria does not need foreign jihadis and radical Islamists—it has more than enough of the home-grown variety. This is where people so often miss the nature of Syria's Muslim Brotherhood, easily the most coherent political force in Syria's opposition today. It is an organization stuck in a time warp from 1982, when it lost the last round of Syria's long civil war, and has been waiting for its chance at revenge. Syria's Muslim Brotherhood is not like its analogues in Egypt, Tunisia, Jordan, or Morocco; it has not been part of the political process for decades, "tamed" by having to get its hands dirty in the everyday stuff of politics. It has been a capital offense to be a member or give any support to the Muslim Brotherhood in Syria for three decades. As a result, the organization is secretive and opaque, and it's not clear how much its cadres inside the country interact with its exiled leadership.

Many of the fighters currently battling the Syrian regime honed their guerrilla skills in Iraq, learning urban combat techniques fighting Americans in Iraq from 2003 to 2007. Those who were not killed in Iraq made their way back to Syria (the largest entry point for foreign jihadis entering Iraq during that war), and have taken up arms against their own regime. Their ability to kill a large number of regime forces from the outset of this current round of civil war is indicative of the skill set they already possessed 19 months ago. The body count of 4:1 during the early months of this civil war—that is, four opponents killed for every soldier killed—is quite good for unorganized insurgent groups.

In fact, the insurgents might be *too* good. Neither Syria nor the region would be well served by a decisive victory by either the Assad regime or by the opposition. Breathless supporters of Syria's revolution need to be careful what they wish for. The most powerful elements of Syria's armed opposition would almost certainly be no friend of liberal democracy were they to seize power for themselves. Consider this: The dissidents who brought down autocratic governments in Egypt and Tunisia, even the political Islamists among them, were far more politically liberal than what we see in Syria. And look at those countries now.

What, then? It is not fashionable to say so, but a negotiated outcome remains the best solution to end the killing and prevent the worst elements from either side ruling Syria. An outright opposition victory would likely produce a momentary air of euphoria before the steep decline toward autocracy and darkness begin.

Periodical and Internet Sources Bibliography

The following articles have been selected to supplement the diverse views presented in this chapter.

Aryn Baker	"Forget Chemical Weapons. Assad Regime Uses Starvation as Tactic Against Rebels," *Time*, October 7, 2013.
Nicholas Blanford	"Kerry Praises Assad for Acting on Syria's Chemical Weapons in 'Record Time,'" *Christian Science Monitor*, October 7, 2013.
Alexander Dziadosz and Stephen Kalin	"Al Qaeda-Linked Group Advances on Syrian Rebels Near Turkey," Reuters, October 2, 2013. www.reuters.com.
Daniel Greenfield	"The Myth of the Moderate Syrian Rebels," *FrontPage*, September 9, 2013. http://frontpagemag.com.
Haaretz	"Russia Says It Has Proof Rebels Behind Deadly Chemical Attack in Syria," September 18, 2013.
Nour Malas	"Syrian Rebels Hurt by Delay," *Wall Street Journal*, September 11, 2013.
Greg Miller	"CIA Ramping Up Covert Training Program for Moderate Syrian Rebels," *Washington Post*, October 2, 2013.
Dan Murphy, as told to Mark Levine	"Behind the Accusations of Rebel Chemical Weapons Use in Syria," *AlJazeera*, October 1, 2013. www.aljazeera.com.
Antonio Pampliega	"Aleppo Stalemate Exhausts Syrian Rebels," *Huffington Post*, October 3, 2013. www.huffingtonpost.com.
Tucker Reals	"Syria Chemical Weapons Attack Blamed on Assad, but Where's the Evidence?," CBS News, August 29, 2013. www.cbsnews.com.

CHAPTER 3

What Is the Status of the Syrian Refugee Crisis?

Chapter Preface

Egypt and Syria have long had close ties. From 1958 to 1961, the two countries even united into a single entity known as the United Arab Republic. Thus, when Syria descended into chaos and civil war in 2011, it was natural for refugees to flee to Egypt. And it was natural for Egyptians to welcome them. Mohamed Morsi, then president of Egypt, decreed that the Syrian refugees should receive free health care and education. Islamic charities provided many of them free apartments. Syrians enjoyed many more benefits and privileges than refugees from places like Somalia who had lived in Egypt much longer, according to journalist Maggie Flick in a September 12, 2013, article for Reuters news service.

The situation for Syrians in Egypt changed drastically in early July 2013, when the Egyptian army staged a coup, forcing Morsi and his Islamist party, the Muslim Brotherhood, out of office. The coup was very divisive, and, according to journalist Peter Schwartzstein in a September 12, 2013, post at the *Atlantic,* "The interim Egyptian government needed a scapegoat to help boost national unity." The Syrians, who had been welcomed by Morsi's government, became that scapegoat.

The government reversed its policy of allowing Syrians to enter the country without visas and took steps to discourage Syrian children from attending Egyptian schools. State media quickly and effectively fanned the hatred. Schwartzstein reports that Tawfiq Okasha, an Egyptian talk show host, has encouraged his listeners to attack Syrian homes. Many Egyptian employers began firing Syrians from their jobs. In a October 6, 2013, post on the *New Republic,* journalist Laura Dean says that she spoke to a nineteen-year-old Syrian who was attacked on the street and had a rope strung around his neck.

Faced with this outpouring of violence and hatred, Syrian refugees had few options. Those with money tried to flee

Egypt. In September 2013, three thousand Syrians arrived in Italy, most of them from Egypt. Dean says that others hoped to move to Sudan, Algeria, or Switzerland. Those unable to leave tried to stay off the streets. Some even talked about going back to Syria, where the war still rages and their lives would be in even more danger. Faced with war at home and persecution abroad, Syrian refugees are caught in an impossible situation.

The viewpoints in this chapter examine other issues confronting Syrian refugees in countries throughout the region, including Lebanon, Iraq, Israel, Jordan, and Turkey.

"Some refugees are being pushed out onto the streets—creating an urban refugee problem that aid agencies warn needs an urgent response."

Analysis: The Syrian Urban Refugee Problem in Northern Iraq

Louise Redvers

Louise Redvers is a journalist, analyst, and translator in the United Arab Emirates. In the following viewpoint, written for the United Nations humanitarian news service IRIN, she reports on the difficulties caused by the influx of refugees into northern Iraq, often referred to as Kurdistan because it is dominated by an ethnic group called the Kurds. She notes that Kurdistan opened its borders generously to Syrian refugees but was ill-equipped to deal with the numbers that arrived. This is especially the case with urban refugees, who have moved into Kurdish cities rather than into camps. She adds that Kurdistan has put some restrictions on border crossings to try to get control of the situation and is looking for more donor aid.

As you read, consider the following questions:

1. How does Kurdistan enable many Syrian refugees to live outside refugee camps, according to Redvers?

2. Why do people assume Kurdistan's booming economy can absorb the refugees economically, and why are they mistaken, according to Redvers?

3. When and where does Kurdistan have restricted border crossings, as reported by the author?

On an empty plot of land in northern Iraq next to a beauty salon and opposite a hotel on Erbil's busy Shoresh Street, Mohammed Hassan sits on a patch of crumpled purple carpet with his wife and their two-year-old son.

Above their heads is a sloping roof of cardboard and blankets, draped over sticks. It offers scant shade from the searing midday sun and their faces are flushed.

Gesturing to a pair of metal crutches on the floor, 24-year-old Hassan peels back his left trouser leg to reveal a reddened, scarred stump.

"I was hit by a bomb in Aleppo," he said, matter-of-factly. "I had the amputation surgery there and then we decided to leave to come to Iraq. There was nothing left and too much violence."

Hassan, who travelled with his brother and family in a group of 11, has joined 153,000 Syrians who have fled across the border to the northern semi-autonomous Kurdistan region of Iraq.

Many have settled at Domiz Camp, around 60km from the border.

But beyond the gates of Domiz, there are an estimated 100,000 Syrian refugees living in towns and cities, around one third of whom live in the capital of Iraqi Kurdistan, Erbil.

More than two years into the Syrian crisis, the cost of rent in Erbil is soaring due to demand from both refugees and expatriate oil workers, and savings and job opportunities are dwindling. As a result, some refugees are being pushed out onto the streets—creating an urban refugee problem that aid agencies warn needs an urgent response before it gets out of hand.

An Overcrowded Refugee Camp

Close to the city of Duhok, Domiz Camp was initially planned for 25,000 people but is now home to more than 60,000, testing sanitation and other services to the limit.

Due to the overcrowded conditions at Domiz, even those in the most desperate conditions in Erbil say they do not want to go back to the camp.

The Kurdistan Regional Government (KRG) in some ways enables this by offering its Syrian refugees renewable six-month work and residency permits. This gives the new arrivals permission to work, access to public health care and education, and freedom of movement, so they are legally allowed to settle in regular communities.

Many of the Syrians arriving in Kurdistan are professionals and most have found work, enabling them to pay for accommodation, or they have found lodgings with friends and family.

Begging for Scraps

But according to the UN Refugee Agency (UNHCR), in Erbil alone there are around 650 families living rough in partly-constructed buildings and makeshift shelters. Many more are sharing rooms in small apartments, bed-hopping between shifts.

"We have people living in unfinished houses, with no doors, walls, windows or roofs, and sometimes there are three families in each room," explained Wiyra Jawhar Ahmed, the manager of the Protection Assistance Reintegration Centre (PARC) in Erbil, run by Swedish NGO Qandil, but mainly funded by UNHCR.

"They are collecting rotten food from outside shops and begging at restaurants for scraps. They are also being in some cases exploited by people here who are giving them work but for very low wages," he added.

Hassan's brother, whose wife and five children occupy a similar stick and blanket shelter 100m away, has found work on a construction site. But Hassan, who was also a labourer in Syria, says he cannot work because of his leg.

For now he is relying on charity from host communities, who on the whole have responded generously to TV and radio campaigns by supporting the refugees with food and bedding.

A KRG official acknowledged that some of the urban refugees may have been equally vulnerable in Syria, but he said they still had the same right to assistance as other refugees.

Stop-Gap Solutions

A new refugee camp was supposed to have opened just outside Erbil in May to accommodate people like Hassan and his family, but funding and planning bottlenecks mean it is not likely to be ready until September.

In the meantime, UNHCR, in conjunction with Qandil, is compiling a database of the most vulnerable urban refugees to whom one-time cash payments of US$225 (paid in two separate installments) are being made available.

So far, of the 250 Erbil refugee families classified as "extremely vulnerable", due to physical disability, chronic illness and other problems, 156 have received money to help pay for healthcare and other basic needs.

Acknowledging this is only a temporary stop-gap, Qandil's Ahmed told IRIN: "It is critical that we get these families into a camp as soon as possible so we can provide them with food, shelter and health care."

He added: "We already have other groups of internally displaced persons (IDPs) here, many from the disputed Nineveh Province, and there are growing tensions with people begging."

Oil-Rich Kurdistan?

Rizgar Mustafa, mayor of Khabat, the district where the new camp will be located, blamed a lack of money for the delayed opening. He said the central government of Iraq in Baghdad had failed to support KRG and that international donor funding had also been slow to arrive.

"There is an assumption that Kurdistan is rich in oil and therefore rich in resources so we can provide for the refugees ourselves," he sighed.

Kurdistan's economy is booming, thanks to a raft of new oil discoveries and a rush of foreign investment, but the oil industry itself is yet to earn money for KRG, amid a long-running dispute about revenue rights with the central government in Baghdad. Kurdistan's current oil production—around 200,000 barrels per day—is one tenth of Nigeria's.

As such, Mustafa said, KRG needs donor funding like any other country dealing with the spillover of the Syrian crisis: "The voice of our government is not as strong as that of Turkey and other established states and we have not received the same response as other places," he said.

As of 22 July, the aid operation in Iraq had received 22 percent of needed funding, compared to 22 percent in Egypt, 25 percent in Turkey, 36 percent in Lebanon and 45 percent in Jordan, according to the latest funding update.

Strategic Approach

But funding is just one part of the picture. Both KRG and UNHCR have come in for criticism for how they have responded to Iraq's urban refugees.

In a report published last month, the Norwegian Refugee Council (NRC) warned that while Iraqi Kurdistan started with a "positive, durable approach" to protect and integrate Syrian refugees, the lack of funding and political and technical support was "presenting substantial economic and social challenges."

Sara Eliasi, a protection and advocacy adviser with NRC, told IRIN: "The government was very willing to receive these refugees but they didn't necessarily envisage or understand the implications and the commitment that it would imply.

"They didn't prepare and they didn't plan for it and unfortunately the international community and international NGOs did not come in and fill that gap and provide a strategic approach."

Prioritizing Urban Refugees

One UNHCR staff member admitted privately: "Urban refugees were not seen as a priority, even though they numbered far more than those in camps, but now we are all working together on a new strategy going forward to address the issues."

Aurvasi Patel, acting head of UNHCR's North of Iraq office, said: "In consultation with the Kurdish authorities, we implemented a joint response to the refugees living in camps as a strategic priority. . . . However, in recognition of the fact that the needs get bigger and that the non-camp refugees were as vulnerable as those living in camps, we started to proportionally direct assistance to ensure an equal response."

Border Closures

Since mid-May, according to UNHCR, the main river crossing point into Iraqi Kurdistan at Peshkapor has been largely restricted.

Dindar Zebari, a senior KRG Foreign Ministry representative, denied the unofficial crossing was totally closed but admitted security had been enhanced.

The Kurds in Northern Iraq

The Kurdish-inhabited region of northern Iraq has been relatively peaceful and prosperous since the fall of [Iraqi dictator] Saddam Hussein [in 2003]. However, the Iraqi Kurds' political autonomy, and territorial and economic demands, have caused friction with Prime Minister Nuri al-Maliki and other Arab leaders of Iraq, and with Christian and other minorities in the north. . . . Turkey and Iran were skeptical about Kurdish autonomy in Iraq but have reconciled themselves to this reality and have emerged as major investors in the Kurdish region of Iraq.

The major territorial, financial, and political issues between the Kurds and the central government do not appear close to resolution. Tensions increased after Kurdish representation in two key mixed provinces was reduced by the January 31, 2009, provincial elections. The disputes nearly erupted into all-out violence between Kurdish militias and central government forces in mid-2009, and the Kurds continue not to recognize the authority of the Sunni Arab governor of Nineveh Province in Kurdish-inhabited areas of the province. . . . The Kurds also perceive that their role as "kingmakers" in Iraq's central government—their ability to throw their parliamentary votes toward one side or another—was reduced by the March 7, 2010 elections which saw the seats held by the major Kurdish factions lowered from previous levels.

Kenneth Katzman,
Congressional Research Service, October 1, 2010.

"There must be clear evidence; those who are crossing the border are very much in need of protection and support," he said.

Al-Qa'im border crossing, controlled by the central government based in Baghdad, has been closed for months.

The closures have sparked outrage from rights groups but officials at Domiz camp have quietly welcomed the time to catch up with camp extension plans that had been constantly on the back foot due to the sheer volume of daily arrivals.

The new camp, known as Dara Shakran, is about 30 minutes' drive north of Erbil and will have an initial capacity of around 10,000, though the final details are still being worked out.

Mayor Mustafa insisted the camp will have no fences and is aimed at providing basic services, not containing the refugees. But some urban refugees may want to stay put.

Community workers have warned this may test the patience of host communities that are increasingly unhappy about the rise in begging and other harmful coping responses such as sex work.

Hassan's sister-in-law, Sharda, a mother of five with the youngest just three months, told IRIN: "If my husband has work here in Erbil, then I won't go to the camp."

"Though the victims [of the Syrian civil war] are seen as 'the enemy,' the question is: 'Can't we let them come here [to Israel] for safe haven?'"

Why Has Israel Closed Its Doors to Syrian Refugees?

Angela Godfrey-Goldstein

Angela Godfrey-Goldstein is a peace activist and an advocacy officer at the Jahalin Association, which works in behalf of the Arab Bedouin tribes displaced by the establishment of the State of Israel in 1948. In the following viewpoint, she asserts that Israel has an honorable history of welcoming refugees but that the government's recent antipathy to Palestinian rights and to its neighbors in the region has resulted in cruel and short-sighted antirefugee policies. She says this is evident most recently in the Israeli refusal to welcome Syrian refugees, which should not be its policy, she concludes.

As you read, consider the following questions:

1. What actions does Godfrey-Goldstein say Menachem Begin took on behalf of refugees?

2. According to the author, why were Israelis flummoxed during the Carmel Fire of 2010?

3. What does Israel see as its mother country, according to Godfrey-Goldstein?

Three questions about the Syrian refugee crisis. First, why is Israel doing nothing?

On our northern border with Syria, within sight of Israeli hikers in the Golan, bombs are to be seen exploding, people running in fear and panic for their lives, as casualties fall. For those watching, though the victims are seen as 'the enemy,' the question is: "Can't we let them come here for safe haven? Can't we do something?" Good questions!

We have indeed traveled a long way since Menachem Begin originally accepted 66, and finally 300, Vietnamese boat-people to Israel in the late 1970s because "we Israelis know what it means to be refugees" and understood the certain death implicit in being refused.

Israel has recently been interning (in terrible conditions), or repatriating, bona fide Eritrean and South Sudanese refugees, currently via Jordan to a third African state; this, despite those refugees having originally faced death in the countries of their origin, and again when returning. Not to mention the excruciating torment of their original flight being repeated, and possibly resulting in capture, rape, torture, imprisonment or even death. On our southern border a huge fence has been hastily constructed to keep such refugees out, even when their presence begging at our gates has been life threatening for them.

As to Syrian refugees, Minister of Defence Ya'alon and Prime Minister Netanyahu have followed their previous form, saying "We have no intention of opening refugee camps" (Ya'alon) and "Israel has maintained that it will not allow refugees into the country, but it has treated a small number of wounded Syrian civilians" (Netanyahu). Both leaders take that position of denial, presumably because they see those ordinary civilian neighbours as enemies, as Arab Muslims, against whom they are waging battles on many fronts and in many guises.

They see themselves fighting demographic warfare whereby the strategic capture of land, or revocation of identity documents disallowing Palestinians from living in East Jerusalem, or from family reconciliation, serve racist goals of containing Palestinians in ever smaller ghettoes or forcing them to leave. But never making peace with them, or treating them as equals. Or reaching out. Or espousing universal values, such as human rights. Oh no.

Tragically for Israel in 2013, Ya'alon and Netanyahu do not, I believe, have the ability to review those attitudes and see that even a goodwill gesture could turn the "game" upside down to Israel's benefit. Were we to cease demonising our neighbours (or indeed all Muslims—including those with whom Israel has peace treaties), and were we to cease seeing this as a zero sum game, but rethink conflict management and opt for conflict resolution, win-win could be our vision. In other words, adopting Syrian refugees, in the spirit in which Begin adopted Vietnamese boat-people, could shift the entire Middle East logjam by galvanising a re-think, and opening our closed minds and cold, selfish, fearful hearts, which cling to our traumas like scabs constantly being scratched off.

No surprise Israelis were totally flummoxed, during the Carmel Fire in 2010, when neighbours actually sent fire-fighting planes to help us. Turkish assistance, especially, came as a huge surprise, since the Mavi Marmara slaughter was still very much a thorn wounding the relationship. Palestinian fire-fighting equipment was of a far higher standard than our own, causing no small embarrassment, especially at a time when the sides were refusing to meet. But no, in the ghetto mentality, one must go it alone against the world. So foolish and so tragic. And in the multi-ethnic world in which we live,

Israel and the Bedouins

Upon becoming a state in 1948, Israel . . . enacted a settlement policy that focused on its nomadic Bedouin in the southern Negev Desert. David Ben-Gurion, Israel's first prime minister, wrote of the government's object: "Negev land is reserved for Jewish citizens whenever and wherever they want. We must expel the Arabs and take their place." Accordingly, 85 percent of the Bedouin population was expelled from the Negev, with only nineteen of the original ninety-five tribes remaining. Many were pushed into Gaza, the West Bank, or across the international borders into Sinai or Jordan.

The entire Southern District incorporating the Negev was placed under military administration, which claimed ownership of all Negev land for the Israeli slate. The remaining Bedouin tribes were relocated to settlements within the Siyag (meaning "fence"), a reservation-like area in the northern Negev of 1,000 square kilometers, about one-tenth of the region. They were relocated for the ultimate purpose of settling and establishing them as an urban population. . . .

While they were eventually granted Israeli citizenship and even served in the Israeli military, the Bedouin, residing in impoverished villages, continued to complain of marginalization and the lack of government services. Many chose to remain on their traditional lands in illegal settlements that were constantly destroyed by the Israeli government.

Akbur Ahmed, The Thistle and the Drone, *2013.*

our colonialism, exceptionalism and racial purity are extraordinarily badly timed! We are really out of step, lagging behind a world that has moved forward. Stubbornly clinging to our victimhood, so that other victims will never qualify for status, and we shall never be part of a normalised world—a world which increasingly has to come together to fight the modern plagues, such as global warming.

Is it defensible?

This attitude may be understandable at a gut level, but is really self-defeating if we aspire to be a humane, compassionate and modern society and not a failed state, banana republic.

As humanitarians we accepted a few Syrian patients to our hospitals, but immediately repatriated them back into the line of fire. Innocent civilians need safe haven. Far wiser to differentiate maturely between ordinary civilians in need, and fighters with whose cause we differ (especially since the Free Syrian rebel army is now constituted of fighters from distant lands fighting proxy wars).

In pursuing this narrow-minded, tribal mindset, where egotistic self-interest is limited to nationalistic politics and short-term goals, we lose track of the basics of Judaism: treat others as you would be treated.

Who is pointing this out?

On September 6th 2012, Lisa Goldman wrote in +972 Mag of Israel's refusal to accept Eritrean refugees:

Today, the government announced that it was allowing three of the refugees—two women and a child—to enter Israel. The other 18 men were turned over to the Egyptians, who may repatriate them to Eritrea. According to Human Rights Watch's reports, those men face indefinite forced army service, torture or jail in their native country. Or perhaps torture and death at the hands of Sinai smugglers who murder refugees in order to reportedly harvest and traffic their organs. In order to save those two women and a child, they basically sacrificed their lives.

According to an Associated Press report about Israel's rescue of the Vietnamese boat people, Menachem Begin agreed to take them in and grant them citizenship after Japan, Taiwan and Hong Kong had refused to accept them. He called their refusal "shameful." Former prime minister Golda Meir added, "Would one not rescue a stray dog or a wounded bird?"

As far as I know, none of the major Jewish organizations have called the Israeli government to task for its deeply shameful and cruel treatment of a little band of Eritrean refugees.

Nor is anyone raising the roof in Israel to demand shelter for some of the million or more Syrian refugees in flight from a land in which over 90,000 have recently died, even when those refugees threaten the viability of neighbouring hosts such as Jordan, in an ever more volatile region. One can only surmise that this lack of commitment comes as a response to the changing demography, in which Israel, although more powerful by far in the Israel-Palestine equation, sees itself as the victim, weak, threatened by millions of hostile neighbours and its agenda dominated by military "wisdom" which increasingly makes us racist, xenophobic, in denial and inhumane.

While Europe and the United States are seen as our mother countries, we long since have turned our backs, with our Iron Wall-, fortress- or ghetto- mentality, on neighbours of the Middle East, whose goings on might as well be taking place on another planet. Indeed, our ghetto mentality precludes involvement in the big bad world around us—far safer to stay alone, hunkered down, sure in the knowledge that they all hate us.

Maybe talkbacks to this article will argue against the impression that no one's pointing out this folly. Israeli activists work with African refugee or migrant worker communities to defend their rights, as indeed does the UN Office of the High

Commissioner for Refugees in Tel Aviv. Yet public silence reigns about the need to host Syrian neighbours urgently in need of haven; if a 'quake struck Damascus, would we not send rescue dogs and field hospitals? Don't ask.

Working with Bedouin refugees from 1951, currently threatened with ongoing forced displacement, one is well aware of traditional hospitality whose greeting "Ahalan wa sahalan" means "our home is your home." But no, Israel 2013 is a state of rejectionism. Just leave us alone. Don't remind us that the status quo is unsustainable, that the world around us is in flux. It's all too much. Just leave us alone to keep on muddling through, miserable in our muddle, with no clarity or leadership to lead us to the promised land. Go look somewhere else, so we can pass the buck. And keep on displacing our own internal refugees, while the international community talks grave breaches, war crimes or crimes against humanity. While we shoot down the messengers of chutzpah, such as UN Special Rapporteur for Human Rights in the OPT, Prof. Richard Falk, for doing his job.

> *"The result [of U.S. failure to aid Syrian rebels] is that refugee camps in Turkey are major breeding grounds for anti-U.S. sentiment."*

Syrian Refugees Entering Turkey Create Dangers for the United States

Mark A. Grey

Mark A. Grey is a professor of anthropology at the University of Northern Iowa and a specialist in immigration and refugee affairs. In the following viewpoint, he contends that Syrian refugees in Turkish camps are angry at the United States for not providing assistance to the rebels in overthrowing Syrian leader Bashar al-Assad. He notes that the Turks have been very generous with refugee aid and that the camps are well built, but the refugee problem is still overwhelming the country's resources. He concludes that the United States must combat the anti-American sentiment by providing aid to the camps or risk creating another generation of terrorists determined to damage the United States.

As you read, consider the following questions:

1. According to Grey, why do Turkish AFAD leaders not use the term *refugee* for Syrians in their country?

Mark A. Grey, "Why Syrians In Turkey Are Not 'Refugees' and Why it Matters," *Small Wars Journal*, August 30, 2013. Copyright © 2013 by Small Wars Journal. All rights reserved. Reproduced by permission.

2. Why does the possible use of refugee camps as military bases stir fear among ordinary Turks, in the author's opinion?

3. What two conspiracy theories from the camps does Grey discuss?

Half a million people have fled the Syrian civil war and now live in Turkey. Thousands live in camps built by the Turkish government but camp administrators refuse to label Syrian occupants as "refugees." Instead, Syrians are "guests" who don't deserve the stigma associated with refugees in the rest of the world. Syrians refuse to call themselves refugees because they are not fleeing a civil war. Instead, they were forced to leave Syria because the United States and other western powers didn't support their rebellion against the al-Assad regime. The result is that refugee camps in Turkey are major breeding grounds for anti-U.S. sentiment. The United States and other western powers need to move quickly to counter these anti-American sentiments and fill a void that is being filled by the Gulf States, including Saudi Arabia. Allowing this anti-American sentiment to ferment has important implications for our future security. By not backing up the Syrian rebellion when we had a chance to, we are creating the next generation of terrorists and thousands of them will live in a NATO [North Atlantic Treaty Organization] nation.

Turkey's Open-Door Policy

Turkey has publically maintained an "open door" policy for Syrians escaping the brutal war between the Free Syrian Army (FSA) and the regime of Bashar al-Assad. At first, these refugees trickled in. The United Nations High Commissioner for Refugees (UNHCR) estimated the number of Syrians crossing into Turkey in May 2011 was only about 250. More than two years later, in August 2013, the Turkish Foreign Ministry estimated the total number of refugees who had registered—or who had appointments to register—reached 458,837 with 200,551 living in camps and about 243,985 living in apartments, with friends or relatives, or in informal camps set up in Turkish border towns. With no end in sight for the war, the UNHCR projected the displacement of 3.5 million Syrians by the end of 2013 with as many as 1 million seeking refuge in Turkey.

Turkey's response to the massive influx of Syrians is admirable. Principally through the work of the Turkish Red Crescent and the Turkish Disaster Emergency Management Presidency (AFAD), 20 camps have been established at a cost of $1.5 billion. Turkey has paid most of the bill. In April of [2013], the International Crisis Group (ICG) referred to the refugee camps in Turkey as the "best refugee camps ever seen." I visited several of the Syrian camps in Turkey as well as refugee camps in many other countries and I have to agree with the ICG assessment. Indeed, some of the Turkish "camps" more closely resemble small cities with families living in prefabricated "containers" complete with running water, sewage and electricity. Food is available in large, well-stocked stores operated by the World Food Program. Mosques, health services, playgrounds, and schools are also established in the camps. Elbeyli, the most recently opened camp, has more than 3,300 containers and the capacity for 30,000 residents. The Elbeyli camp director is not a refugee specialist but a city planner.

Turkey's Long-Term Refugee Problem

The high quality of Turkey's refugee camps (and the accommodation of Syrians in cities) does not solve the nation's long-term refugee problem. By any definition, the Syrian newcomers are "refugees." They clearly fit the United Nations definition as people who have "a well-founded fear of being persecuted for reasons of race, religion, nationality, membership of a particular social group or political opinion," they have crossed an international border, and they are unable to return home. Despite this legal description of the Syrians in Turkey, the Syrians—and many Turks—reject the label. There are many reasons for this and more importantly, there are short- and long-term consequences for the Turks, Syrians, and American foreign policy.

An Obligation as Hosts

I met several Turkish AFAD leaders, camp directors, and educators and they did not like the term "refugee" for a few reasons. One issue is that the word "refugee" translates into Turkish (mülteci) not as one who seeks refuge but as "one who dwells." The Syrians are not refugees but guests and given the cultural pride Turks take in hosting their guests, AFAD leaders feel an obligation to host Syrians in the best facilities they can provide. As one AFAD director told me, the nicest room in the house is always reserved for providing hospitality.

As a Muslim nation, Turkey also has an obligation to welcome fellow Muslims who are never strangers but fellow members of the same *Ummah* or community of Muslims. Less often expressed, but underlying the motivations of many relief workers, is Turkey's obligation as a predominately Sunni nation to welcome the predominately Sunni flow of Syrians. The majority of Syrians in the camps are Sunni. In order to avoid conflict in the crowded camps, those who are not Sunnis either claim they are Sunni or they don't identify themselves. Anticipating problems with large influxes of Alawite Muslims and Christians in Sunni-dominated camps, AFAD is building two new separate camps for these two special populations.

Turkish Camps Are at Capacity

Despite the Turkish investment in refugee facilities and its "open door" rhetoric, the country has probably met its capacity to help Syrians. Turkey has offered to airlift refugees to Europe. So far there have been few takers, although Canada announced its willingness to resettle 1,500. There are more ominous signs: This summer Human Rights Watch claimed Turks are now refusing to admit all but a few Syrians, leaving thousands stranded in make-shift camps along the Syrian side of the border.

Although AFAD camp directors may claim an obligation to welcome the Syrians, popular Turkish resentment against the influx is growing. In towns near the border, there are complaints about how much public funding goes into building, securing, staffing and maintaining the camps. The electric bill for the Kilis container camp alone runs about 1.5 million Turkish lire (about $900,000) per month. With limited contributions from other nations, all of the Turkish money spent on Syrian camps, schools, clinics, and personnel is money that is not spent on Turks and their children.

Syrians are registered by the Turkish government but the majority of them are not allowed to work. As more of them live in towns and are desperate for incomes, employers are taking advantage of them with long hours and at wages lower than those expected by Turks. Many are paid in cash. Some camp dwellers are also allowed to work on occasion as temporary farm workers. Turks also complain about a shortage of housing and upward pressure on rents. And there are persistent—although unfounded—rumors that Syrians are also involved in prostitution, human trafficking, pick-pocketing, and human organ trafficking.

Turks Fear Spillover of War

Turkish fears that the conflict in Syria may spill over the border are augmented by growing recognition that the refugee camps are used as bases by members of the FSA where they rest, visit family, receive health care, and obtain supplies. Turkish border guards allow their free flow back and forth across the border. Security at camp gates varies in terms of the quality of personnel and security procedures. Persistent rumors that the camps are used as rebel bases were confirmed in the April 2013 International Crisis Group report, noting that allowing the use of camps as bases threatens to exacerbate "sensitive ethnic and sectarian balances, particularly in Hatay province" where a significant proportion of the population are Alawites who share more ethnic and cultural ties with fellow Shia Alawites in Syria than with Sunni Turks.

The use of refugee camps as military bases also strikes at the very principles upon which services for refugees are provided: Refugees don't go back and forth to their home country to fight; they seek refuge in another nation and hope someday they can go home. Using camps as military bases also stirs fears among ordinary Turks that the war will cross into their territory. In light of how camps are used as bases, ICG's recommendations to the Turkish government are direct and leave no room for doubt: "Minimise border crossings by Syrian opposition fighters; do not allow them to use refugee camps as rear bases; ensure there is no pressure on young camp residents to join opposition militias; and establish new refugee camps well away from the border."

"Don't Call Us Refugees"

AFAD Camp directors and common Turks are reluctant to call Syrians "refugees" and the Syrians I met also deeply dislike the label. This point was driven home several times when, through an interpreter, I used the word "refugee" and was immediately admonished. Some Syrians do not want to be wrapped up in the same negative status as refugees in other parts of the world, especially in Africa. Their resistance to the "refugee" label also reflected their beliefs that Muslims are not refugees in the nations of other Muslims but "guests." Some preferred the term "temporary asylum seeker." At the request of camp education directors, I provided training for camp teachers on refugee trauma. Many Syrians rejected the existence of trauma in their population because only true refugees suffer from trauma and admitting that Syrians experience trauma would make them refugees, too. In other instances, Syrians described behaviors among their children and parents that are clearly linked to their war and migration experiences, but they argued devout Muslims do not need to treat for trauma because all the treatment they need is found in the [Muslim holy book] Quran and Hadiths [sayings of the Prophet Muhammad].

There were other reasons why Syrians reject the refugee label. Many Syrians in the camps said they were not refugees because they are not like the refugee populations living in Syria. The Palestinians, Iraqis and Lebanese who live in Syria were true refugees because they were victims of civil war. The Syrians in Turkey, on the other hand, are not victims of civil war but rather a revolution for freedom: a righteous rebellion, an uprising of oppressed peoples much like those experienced throughout the Arab Spring. The only reason they had to leave Syria and seek temporary asylum in Turkey was because the United States and other Western powers failed to support their uprising. In other words, they are not truly refugees because the lack of U.S. military support forced them to leave Syria. When the armed rebellion began in March 2011, the Syrians I met expected rapid and decisive U.S. intervention like that provided in Libya. When that didn't happen, and as losses of life and property mounted, people fled Syria not because they had started a civil war and found themselves losing, but because the Americans didn't show up when they were supposed to.

Anti-U.S. Anger and Resentment

The resulting anger and resentment against the U.S. and other Western powers ferments in the camps and grows deeper with each week the U.S. doesn't intervene. It is exacerbated by what the refugees see as western double standards and how the "red line" drawn by President [Barack] Obama to intervene if the Assad regime used chemical weapons has moved several times.

They also readily dismiss as an "excuse" the reluctance of Americans to provide heavy and sophisticated weapons to the Syrian rebels because of concerns about arming more radical Islamist elements. Most of the Syrians I talked to, including many who have or continue to fight, told me the percentage of rebels aligned with al-Nusra or other groups associated with al Qaeda was really only two or three percent, much lower than claimed by the United States. The U.S. is exaggerating to avoid living up to their moral commitment. Many Syrians also discount American concerns about infighting among factions of the FSA—as well as posted YouTube videos of rebels beheading Catholic priests—as a stalling tactic.

Their anti-American sentiment is at times as harsh as their feelings for al-Assad and it is very personal. They have lost their homes, careers, and family members and find themselves living in crowded camps in a country where they don't speak the language and can't work. Being called "refugees" is the last straw.

Whatever aid was provided by the United States prior to August 2013 is shrugged off as piece-meal or meaningless. Even though I believe most of the Syrians I met are grateful to the Turkish government for building camps and providing safe sanctuaries for themselves and their families, they also deeply resent having to rely on the Turks for historic and cultural reasons. They are unhappy with the Turkish practice of mixing genders in classrooms and workplaces. And, after all, the Turks have also talked about ousting Assad but the Turks have not backed the FSA with anything other than logistical support, medical supplies and light arms.

Why It Matters

There are two principal reasons why Syrians' long-term status as "refugees" matters to Turkey and U.S. foreign policy. The war is very likely to rage on and a half-million or more Syrians in Turkey may not be going home for years or ever. For Turkey, there are potentially devastating consequences. Already pushed to its limits, AFAD and the Turkish government have recently asked for more foreign aid and they will make it easier for foreign Non-Governmental Organizations (NGOs) to work in Turkey. This will help with the present crisis but the long-prospects for Syrian settlement do not bode well for the country. In effect, it would mean that several hundred thousand guests would become permanent residents, the bulk of whom don't speak Turkish. Many professionals from Syria like doctors, professors and engineers will not have their licenses accepted by Turkish authorities. Students from Syrian schools and universities won't have their curricula or diplomas recognized. Schools provided in the camps don't have curricula officially sanctioned or recognized by Turkish education authorities. To make matters even worse, several hundred thousand people would come onto the Turkish labor market where many Turks already fear high unemployment and downward pressure on wages.

Refugees and Anti-Americanism

The thousands of Syrians who may end up living in Turkey for years to come will also harbor lingering anger at the U.S. and other Western powers for their inaction during the war. Many may also blame the Turks for their own inaction. What is clear is that the refugee camps in Turkey are becoming breeding grounds for anti-U.S. sentiment. Living in crowded camps and unemployed, Syrian men and women have little to do but watch political events on satellite television and debate their meaning. (Many of individual tents and containers in the camps have satellite dishes and televisions. There are also separate rooms where men and women gather to watch Arabic-language television networks.) They also have a lot of time to discuss why the west has failed them. The result is a number of conspiracy theories that, in the absence of facts to the contrary, explain U.S. dithering.

Here are two of the prevailing conspiracy theories in the camps. The first is that when all is said and done, the United States and the E.U. [European Union] powers will give up on the rebellion and side with al-Assad whom the west and Israel see as the lesser of two evils: a fractured Syria run in part by Islamists or a whole Syria, returned to the control of a dictator, but one on whom the West can rely to stabilize the region. The second major theory proves the first: The U.S. has officially designated Hezbollah [a militant Islamic Lebanese organization] as a terrorist organization for quite some time but when Hezbollah joined the al-Assad forces to capture Qusair from the rebels in May 2013, the U.S. and Europe gave them a pass. So, as goes this narrative, it must be true that the U.S. was never going to properly back the rebels in the first place and they will give in to Russian pressure to keep al-Assad in power. One man I met in the camps put it this way: "I just wanted to make a better world for me and my children. But now I'm the terrorist and Hezbollah gets to march through Syria and the U.S. does nothing!"

In the final analysis, the United States and other western powers need to move very fast to counter these anti-American sentiments by providing direct aid in the camps and filling a void that is already being filled by other nations, including several from the Gulf States but in particular Saudi Arabia. The consequences of allowing this anti-American sentiment to ferment were made very clear to me by some Syrians in the camps: By not backing up the rebellion when we had a chance to, we are creating the next generation of terrorists and thousands of them—unemployed and unemployable—will live in a NATO nation.

> *"Camps . . . engender near-complete dependency and can create tensions between host-country nationals and refugees that jeopardize the well-being of both."*

Camps Are a Poor Way to House Syrian Refugees

Refugees International

Refugees International (RI) advocates for protection for displaced peoples. In the following viewpoint, the organization reports on the Syrian refugee situation in Turkey and Jordan. It asserts that the situation is increasingly difficult and argues that refugees need to be allowed to leave camps and seek out jobs and other opportunities. It contends that restricting refugees to camps limits their independence and freedom and concludes that more aid and support is needed for refugees who are not in camps. This viewpoint is excerpted and adapted from the organization's full report.

As you read, consider the following questions:

1. In what ways does RI say that the situation facing Syrians varies from country to country?

2. What document pertaining to refugees has the Turkish government not made public, according to the author?

3. What problems does RI identify with the Zaatari camp in Jordan?

The civil war in Syria has forced large numbers of Syrians from their homes, and in many cases from the country entirely. Refugees continue to flee in record numbers, and there are currently almost 400,000 registered or waiting for registration in Iraq, Jordan, Lebanon, and Turkey combined. The United Nations has said it expects this number could reach 700,000 by December 31, 2012. About half of all the registered Syrians are living in camps, but the other half remain in local host communities trying to get by on their own.

Alternatives to Camps Are Needed

In October 2012, Refugees International [RI] spent several weeks visiting Syrian refugee camps and urban Syrian refugee populations in Turkey, Jordan, and Iraq. The situation facing Syrians varies from country to country. For example, in Turkey, many of the refugees, aid workers, and activists RI interviewed said that the Turkish government's camps are acceptable, even if not ideal. In Jordan and Iraq, the camps need improvement, but people living in them can obtain minimal services. A major challenge that exists in all three countries, however, is the specific vulnerability of urban Syrian refugee populations.

Many of the Syrians who now live in neighboring countries brought some financial resources with them, but these will not last long—and for many families, they have already run out. Once they are unable to obtain shelter on their own, they face a stark choice: either move to a camp for assistance, or struggle through the winter in urban areas where there is very little support and where the numbers of Syrian refugees needing help get larger and larger. Though urban refugees generally also need assistance with the costs of food, medical care, and transportation, their most pressing need is often maintaining their residence so that the alternative (relocating to a camp) does not become necessary.

The camps in all three countries RI visited are already at capacity or overcrowded, with more Syrians crossing the border every day or moving in from urban areas. These camp residents are not always free to come and go as they see fit— whether for work, specialized medical care, or to visit family. But as the attached reports make clear, each country also faces its own unique problems in dealing with fleeing Syrians. Thousands are stuck inside Syria, just beyond the Turkish border, where they are waiting for the Turkish government to build more accommodations and let them in. Service providers in the Jordanian and Iraqi camps are struggling to meet even the most basic protection needs, such as registration and emergency medical care. In all three countries, circumstances are already extremely difficult for both refugees and service providers, but the lack of progress toward a political settlement in Syria points toward even further deterioration.

While camps may make it easier for governments and aid agencies to locate, register, and protect people by keeping them in a defined location, they also prevent people from being as self-sufficient as possible.

Living outside of camps in host communities can afford refugees opportunities to work and provide for themselves, to learn new skills, and to develop support networks in a community. All of these facilitate reintegration—in this case, return to Syria—when the time comes, as people will have resources to take back with them. Life outside a camp also helps maintain dignity by offering people a more independent life. The Syrian refugee camps in all three countries RI visited are either at or over capacity and cannot keep up with the pace of

Syrian Refugees

Cumulative number of refugees by month, as of March 12, 2014. Includes people registered and awaiting registration.

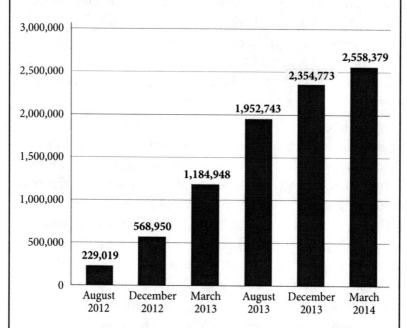

Note: Data from US Department of State, Humanitarian Information Unit. February 2013 includes Egypt. March 2013 onward includes North Africa.

TAKEN FROM: ReliefWeb, "Syria: Numbers and Locations of Refugees and IDPs," August 2012–March 2014. http://reliefweb.int.

arrivals. For all of these reasons, it is essential that assistance programs support the integration of refugees into non-camp situations whenever possible.

Turkey's Response

Since the beginning of the conflict in Syria in early 2011, Turkey has done an admirable job of receiving and hosting Syrian refugees using its own financial and human resources. There are now over 120,000 Syrian refugees registered in the country, most of whom live in one of 14 camps spread out across the southeast. The Turkish government did not allow RI access to any of these refugee camps, but they are generally acknowledged to provide adequate services and acceptable living conditions. However, the situation for Syrian refugees living outside the camps in Turkey is quite different. Support for this population is practically non-existent, and the government of Turkey should offer assistance in order to prevent people from having to relocate to a camp—where they would prefer not to live—in order to seek help.

For almost two years, Turkey has kept its border open to Syrians fleeing the conflict in their country. Turkish law provides temporary asylum on an individual basis to non-European refugees entering its territory. Faced with the mass influx of Syrians fleeing conflict, Turkey established a group designation called temporary protection. Reportedly, under an April 2012 government directive, this designation allows Syrian refugees to enter Turkey and prohibits their forced return to Syria. However, it remains unclear how temporary protection applies to Syrians living outside the camps.

The principle of temporary protection for Syrians who enter camps after crossing the border allows them to register with the Turkish government and receive support within the confines of the camp. There are no questions about their status or whether or not they are eligible for help, and it is clear that they cannot be returned to Syria against their will. The camps themselves are at capacity, and there are thousands of people being held up on the Syrian side of the border until more accommodation can be built. Turkey appears willing to accept them as space becomes available and to address their humanitarian needs—like shelter, food, and medical attention—all under the auspices of providing temporary protection.

However, there are now also tens of thousands of Syrians living in cities and towns with few options for support, since there is no social services network available to them. They are not able to register with the Turkish government or the UN Refugee Agency (UNHCR) because such a process does not exist outside the camps. They must pay independently for rent, food, and health care. And as their savings dwindle, their main option for obtaining help is to move into one of the camps.

The Turkish government has offered no official guidance as to how the temporary protection policy applies to Syrian refugees outside the camps, and the rights and responsibilities of these non-camp Syrians remain unclear. It is generally understood that they cannot be returned to Syria, but their humanitarian needs like shelter and food are not being addressed by any agency. Furthermore, there is no consistent guidance on whether or not they can officially maintain legal residence in Turkey outside the camps. As a result, they live in constant fear of having to move to a camp, where they would be separated from whatever family, friends, and support they may have in the cities. The Turkish government issued a directive in April 2012 on how the temporary protection policy applies to different categories of Syrian refugees, but it has not been made public and therefore offers no practical guidance for government officials, service providers, and refugees themselves. The Turkish government should immediately make public the April 2012 directive and should provide official guidance as to how the policy applies to Syrians outside of the camps.

Outside the Camps

There is no officially-accepted data on how many Syrians are living outside the camps in Turkey. This is partly because refugees in a community setting cannot register for assistance, and partly because some do not want to come forward and reveal their identity or location. Best guesses, however, put the number at about 70,000. These are people who rent residences and meet all their daily needs independently. If they need medical help then they must pay for it at the rates for private care; if they need trauma counseling for the children then they must find and pay for it on their own; and when the prices of rent and food rise they must somehow find a way to adjust.

The ability to register with an organization that can identify a refugee's particular needs and help them find assistance is one of the most basic protection measures in any setting. By creating a record of who is present and what makes them vulnerable, humanitarian aid agencies can understand how many people are in need, where they are located, and what specific services are most essential. While the absence of support services for the urban Syrian refugee population is alarming, those services cannot be developed without first having a clear understanding of who is present and what their needs are. Registration—either in a camp, or in an urban setting—is one of the simplest ways to begin assessing the condition of a population and developing lifesaving responses. This is particularly important with a refugee flow as large and constantly-fluctuating as the Syrian one. The Turkish government, in coordination with the UNHCR, must establish a registration process for refugees living outside of the camps.

Refugee Services

The refugee camps run by the Turkish government allow Syrians access to services that address their basic protection and survival needs. More than that, they offer routine medical care, education, ways to reunite families who have been separated, and opportunities for social interactions that help refugees maintain their mental well-being. In many settings, such assistance also exists through networks of service organizations in urban areas; in Turkey, however, there are none.

Some enterprising Syrian refugees in Turkish cities and towns have created their own aid networks. They do their best to help meet the financial and material needs of their population, to establish educational programs for both children and adults, and to provide a community atmosphere in which people can find emotional support and feel safe in a new and unfamiliar place. But the size of these groups is limited by the financial resources of the people who create them. Once the money runs out, these Syrian refugees lose their support system, and it is at this point that many have to make the difficult decision to move into a camp to survive.

Refugees who do not live in camps generally have some advantages over those who do. Besides maintaining a higher degree of independence, they may be able to earn money, learn skills, remain with a supportive community, and be able to contribute to the host community as well. These individuals then have an easier transition when they are able to return to their own country, as they have been active in sustaining themselves on a daily basis and have maintained those abilities. This is important both for refugee return, and for the rebuilding of a country when it is able to receive its population safely.

While in Turkey, the RI team met Syrian refugees who were suffering for a variety of reasons. Some had tourist visas that were about to expire but were afraid to ask the police for advice because of their uncertain status under temporary protection. Some had serious medical problems but could not go to the hospital because of the expense. Some lacked things as basic as food and clothing and had to rely on the goodwill of neighbors. All were understandably anxious at the prospect of moving to a crowded camp and losing their autonomy, but none could see any other option short of going back to Syria. The Turkish government should establish services for these urban refugees, or else allow other groups to establish them.

Close to 130,000 Syrian refugees are already living in government-run camps in Turkey, and yet Syrians continue to approach the Turkish border in record numbers. Approximately 10,000 are held upon the Syrian side of the Turkey-Syria border, and they will be allowed to cross only after the Turkish government has constructed a physical space where they can live—in essence, a space in a camp. In addition to this large vulnerable group waiting at the border, urban refugees in Turkey suffer from a complete lack of services and assistance that in many cases will eventually drive them into the camps as well. In order to ensure the protection of Syrian refugees, and to provide support in more than just words, the Turkish government must define its temporary protection policy—particularly as it applies to Syrians outside the camps. This policy must then be further bolstered by allowing urban Syrian refugees to register and receive humanitarian assistance through either the Turkish government or the UNHCR.

Jordan

The number of Syrian refugees living in Jordan has swelled to over 100,000 and continues to increase. As they cross the border, many Syrians are being directed into the Zaatari camp, where conditions and services fail to meet international standards. Simultaneously, host communities who have welcomed refugees are under increasing pressure because of the need to share limited resources with their guests. Jordan's border remains open in a clear demonstration of the government's humanitarian commitment towards Syrian refugees. But without greater technical and financial assistance from the international community, these Syrians will be less welcome by host communities and will face more insecurity.

An RI team visited Jordan in June 2012 and observed many Syrian refugees going into Jordanian host communities, while a smaller number remained in the transit centers for long periods. At that time, there were three transit centers at the northern border where arriving Syrians could receive shelter, food, and medical care. After being screened, these individuals were released through a sponsor living in Jordan. The transit centers have since been closed and a camp (Zaatari) has opened instead. When RI returned to Jordan in October, most Syrians arriving at the border were being directed to the camp, where they could receive some assistance but usually not leave. This policy of funneling new arrivals to the camp limits their mobility and self-sufficiency, and large numbers of refugees have left the camp without permission—sometimes even to return to Syria. While camps can help governments and agencies keep track of who is in the country and what their needs are, they engender near-complete dependency and can create tensions between host-country nationals and refugees that jeopardize the well-being of both.

Protection Policy

Once a Syrian refugee has crossed the border into Jordan, the Jordanian police take their identity documents and the refugee receives only a receipt for having turned them over. It is not clear that refugees are able to retrieve their documents upon request. Thus, Syrians who decide to leave the Zaatari camp sometimes do so without any form of documentation. Those who are desperate enough to return to Syria without identification will be even more vulnerable to abuse. This problem is compounded by the fact that more and more refugees are attempting to leave the camp due to poor conditions. Zaatari is hot and dusty during the day, overcrowded, and has inadequate shelter for the approaching winter. Moreover, camp rules prevent residents from leaving the camp to find work. The process that used to allow Syrians to leave the transit centers is used much more selectively in the camp, and now a person can only leave for urgent humanitarian reasons, such as a medical emergency. In one Jordanian hospital, RI met a group of family members who had been transferred out of the camp for specialized health care, but had to leave their 13- and 11-year-old daughters behind without a guardian. Repeated requests to reunite the minors with their family were refused because this did not qualify as an urgent humanitarian situation. The Jordanian government should allow Syrians entering the country with documents to retain them in order to minimize cases like these, and to reduce the risk of Syrians being undocumented when leaving the camp.

Zaatari camp is located not far from a small Jordanian town, yet its tens of thousands of residents are stuck living in tents in a restricted area of the desert. The majority use communal latrines, showers, and kitchens. In addition to the tensions that often arise when people are in such cramped quarters, conditions in the camp are clearly unacceptable in many ways. Camp medical services are quite developed and residents can be referred out for specialized care. However, the elementary school is significantly overcrowded, the child-friendly spaces are desolate, the women's center is located on the periphery of the camp and is difficult to find, and the refugees are not free to seek work or other accommodations outside the camp. Many Syrians departed "unofficially" after the situation became too difficult to endure. During RI's visit, a group of about 15 family members was preparing to leave Zaatari and return to Syria. When asked about this decision, they acknowledged that they did not feel safe returning. They maintained, however, that they could no longer handle daily life in the camp and would rather face the hardships at home. Aid organizations are working hard in the camp to identify needs and provide support, but the constant new arrivals and lack of capacity make it difficult for them to keep up with the work.

Outside the Jordanian Camp

For those Syrians who have been living in urban settings in Jordan for some time (and for the few recent arrivals who have been able to avoid going to Zaatari), the host community is becoming increasingly unwelcoming. Refugees are eligible for services at a number of medical clinics and children have been allowed to enroll in the public school system where there is space. However, the price of rent and food is high, and more than anything people need rental assistance to retain their living quarters. A handful of international organizations provide some financial support for rent and living expenses, but only a small fraction of the urban population receives this help; the rest are on their own. As Syrians run out of savings to sustain them in Jordan, more and more of them are moving to Zaatari to seek out the services they need. To avoid further swelling the camp population, aid agencies should start by distributing rental assistance to the wider urban population. Food and household items must also be offered to larger numbers of people, along with winterization materials like heaters and fuel. The Jordan Hashemite Charity Organization, which coordinates the government's response to Syrian refugees, should prioritize this type of assistance for larger numbers of urban refugees.

Jordan has any number of humanitarian organizations that are equipped and eager to assist Syrian refugees. Unfortunately, the U.S. Department of State, the core donor to these local aid groups, has provided little in the way of new funding to these service providers. Funding for local NGOs [nongovernmental organizations] serving Syrian refugees was limited to $3 million and four organizations across the region in 2012. As a result, Syrians seeking to remain in urban settings can access few services. As greater numbers of Syrian refugees flee the conflict, services that allow individuals to live with minimal assistance outside of camps have become increasingly scarce. In interviews, RI learned that several organizations have been forced to make a hard choice about whom to assist, as they cannot afford to support both camp and urban populations. The U.S. Bureau of Population, Refugees, and Migration (PRM) and European donors should increase funding to inter-governmental and non-governmental organization partners operating in Jordan, both in the Zaatari camp and urban settings.

Since RI's previous visit in June 2012, little has improved for Syrian refugees in Jordan. In fact, some aspects of the situation are worse. There is now a camp housing tens of thousands, services in that camp are inadequate, fewer people are allowed out into the host community, and services for urban refugees are still lacking. Even those who do live in host communities are finding that tensions with Jordanians have increased. The Jordanian government is to be commended for keeping its border open. However, in order to maintain this policy and minimize the strain on the host community, Jordan must receive better support in providing adequate services for both urban Syrian refugees and their Jordanian neighbors.

> "Refugee camps have gotten a bad repu-
> tation as places of insecurity, depen-
> dency and de-humanization. But camps
> provide necessary services to people in
> need."

Refugee Camps Provide Needed Aid and Services

Elizabeth Ferris

Elizabeth Ferris is the codirector of the Brookings-LSE Project on Internal Displacement, a senior fellow in foreign policy at Brookings, and the author of The Politics of Protection. *In the following viewpoint, she addresses a number of difficult issues facing the humanitarian community in light of the Syrian crisis. She asserts that the community needs to reconsider its opposition to refugee camps. She also argues against referring to affected communities as "host countries", and highlights security issues facing countries that take in refugees.*

As you read, consider the following questions:

1. Which country accepting Syrian refugees is a signatory to the UN Refugee Convention, as stated by Ferris?

2. Why does the author say that Lebanon and Jordan are not actually "hosts"?

3. What evidence does Ferris provide that refugees do not always spread violence across borders?

The speed at which Syria's humanitarian crisis is unfolding is breathtaking. In the space of 18 months, Lebanon's refugee population increased from 2,000 to over 500,000—and this in a country with a population of 4 million. Refugees continue to pour across the borders (where they are still able to do so), the international community is mobilizing funds and redeploying staff to the region, and delegations of all sorts are turning up daily in neighboring countries. There is no end in sight to the conflict which has already uprooted over 6 million Syrians—one in three of the country's pre-crisis population. In fact, on a recent trip to the region, everyone we talked with believed that the humanitarian situation would only get much worse.

Fundamental Humanitarian Questions

Governments in the region, international agencies and local civil society groups are all running at full speed to try to keep up with the current challenges. But the Syrian crisis raises some fundamental questions for the humanitarian community which deserve some reflection—even in the midst of the urgency to respond.

1. How do we protect asylum space? Presently, the Lebanese border is open to all Syrian refugees. Until May [2013] the Jordanian border was largely open to Syrians (except for restrictions upon single young men and Palestinians), although since then, it appears that the government has limited the number of Syrians allowed to enter the country. The Turkish government 'manages' its border, limiting the number of Syrian refugee arrivals in accord with camp capacity. The Iraqi border is closed. Even though these governments are not sig-

natories to the 1951 UN Refugee Convention (except for Turkey, although it maintains a restriction allowing only Europeans to be considered refugees), permitting desperate Syrians to cross one's border in search of protection is the right thing to do. Governments in the region deserve the support and gratitude of the international community. But that only goes so far. As my colleague Kemal Kirişci has written, the Turkish government is growing weary of expressions of appreciation and wants more tangible (i.e. financial) support. Countries hosting refugees are bearing a tremendous burden with mounting economic, social, political and security concerns. Beyond expressions of appreciation and financial support, how can the international community support host governments to allow Syrian refugees to remain? Is it just the responsibility of the humanitarian agencies? What about international financial institutions?

Reconsidering Camps

2. Is it time to reconsider the question of camps for refugees? For the past decade or so, the international community seems to have adopted the mantra that people are better off living in host communities than in refugee camps. Refugee camps have gotten a bad reputation as places of insecurity, dependency and de-humanization. But camps provide necessary services to people in need. Even Za'atari camp in Jordan (which is an awful place) provides food, water, health care and shelter—largely in line with international standards. Camps also provide accountability. If a camp fails to provide health care to its residents, it's clear who is to blame. If a Syrian refugee living in an abandoned building can't access a Lebanese hospital, it's less clear who is responsible. The refugee may not know where to go or be unable to pay the bill or the bus fare to get there or be afraid to even leave the apartment. Camps also provide visibility; they are more accessible to media and visiting delegations. Host governments can point to a camp and say 'look

what we're doing.' It's more difficult to be reminded of the burden posed by refugees when they are living in hundreds of different places. In the case of Lebanon where refugees are presently dispersed in more than 1400 sites—many of which are clearly sub-standard—camps are probably a better solution for most, certainly for those living in 'informal tented settlements' as they are euphemistically called. Not only would camps make it easier for international agencies to provide services, but they would be a visible reminder of the refugees' presence in Lebanon. It is simply easier to get media coverage when there is a refugee camp to visit than when it's necessary to seek out individual refugee families living in abandoned buildings or in six-story walk-up apartment buildings.

3. How can the civilian nature of refugee camps be maintained? It is no secret that the Free Syrian Army uses Za'atari refugee camp in Jordan for recruitment, medical care and R&R [rest and rehabilitation] for its soldiers. Nor is it a secret that criminal gangs exercise powerful influence over the camp's economic life and that camp residents sometimes threaten staff. A recent report noted that even the Jordanian teachers don't feel safe in Za'atari classrooms. Everyone seems to recognize the urgent need for increased security in the camp—both for residents and for staff—but there are no easy answers. Dislodging powerful interests that have become entrenched is difficult and dangerous; the commitment of the Jordanian government and police is urgently needed. While it's perhaps easy for an outsider to conclude that the present situation is unacceptable, it is also important to underscore that the negative consequences of a lack of security in Za'atari extend far beyond Jordan's borders—particularly for governments which are considering establishing camps. What government in its right mind would want another Za'atari on its territory?

Reconsidering the Term *Host*

4. Is it time to reconsider the word 'host?' When governments allow refugees to enter their territory, it's fair to refer to them

as 'host governments' (although the phrase doesn't work for those displaced within their country's border.) But the term 'host communities' is more problematic. If you think about it, the word 'host' implies both choice and hospitality. To use a personal example, I host people for dinner—I've invited them, I'm glad to have them in my home. I hosted my cousins visiting Washington last year—they said they'd like to come and I was delighted to have them for a few days (but note that both my dinner guests and my cousins did leave after enjoying my hospitality.) For communities in Lebanon and Jordan, there is often neither choice nor hospitality. Refugees arrive in Lebanese villages and Jordanian communities without having been invited by those communities, and while many—perhaps most—were initially received with great hospitality, the welcome is wearing thin. The refugees can't go home and there is uncertainty over when they will be able to leave. The term 'host community' seems to imply a positive reception of the refugees—or at least a tolerance of their presence—which shouldn't be assumed, particularly as time goes by. The term 'affected community' is perhaps more accurate.

5. Finally, how do we recognize the security implications posed by the presence of refugees while continuing to affirm their basic rights? I've always resisted arguments that refugees are responsible for the spread of violence across borders. For example, in spite of the many dire predictions that Iraqi refugees would bring turmoil to the countries where they sought protection, this didn't happen. Lebanon, on the other hand, worries me. The arrival of over 500,000 Syrian Sunni refugees in a country with a population of 4 million and an unstable government is a security threat. There have been rockets launched from Syria into Hezbollah [a militant Islamic group] territory, there are almost daily armed skirmishes in Tripoli and last week, new outbreaks of fighting occurred in Sidon. In at least some cases, this fighting has included newly-arrived Syrians in the country. Perhaps these incidents would have all

occurred without the presence of the refugees, but the growing number of Syrians in Lebanon is definitely causing tension—between refugees and the communities where they are living; between supporters and opponents of the Assad regime; and between Lebanese sectarian groups and their militias. This affects Lebanon's political future but also affects the Syrian refugees who left Syria to escape armed conflict. There are troubling reports of Syrian refugees in Lebanon who have been displaced two or three times by the violence taking place in their country of refuge.

Periodical and Internet Sources Bibliography

The following articles have been selected to supplement the diverse views presented in this chapter.

Laura Dean	"Syrian Refugees in Egypt: The Unluckiest People on Earth," *New Republic*, October 6, 2013.
Lyse Doucet	"Destitution Drives Syrian Refugee Children to Work," *BBC News*, September 25, 2013. www.bbc.co.uk.
Rebecca Gang	"Syrian Refugees in Iraq Risking Lives to Return Home amid Funding Shortfall," *Guardian*, August 30, 2013.
Azeem Ibrahim	"Syria's Agony in Numbers: The Growing Refugee Crisis," *Huffington Post*, October 4, 2013. www.huffingtonpost.com.
Tom Kutsch	"Syrian Refugees Top 2 Million as Thousands Flee Daily," *Al Jazeera*, September 3, 2013. http://america.aljazeera.com.
Sebastian Meyer	"Syrian Kurdish Refugees Fear Harsh Winter in Northern Iraq," *Voice of America*, October 7, 2013. www.voanews.com.
Peter Schwartzstein	"Egypt's Latest Conspiracy Theories Target the Country's Syrian Refugees," *The Atlantic*, September 12, 2013.
Jeff Tyler	"Jordan Hosts Syria Refugees but Feels the Strain," *Marketplace*, September 12, 2013. www.marketplace.org/
Benjamin Weinthal	"Syrian Refugees Face an Increasingly Horrific Situation in Turkey," *The Atlantic*, October 2, 2013.

CHAPTER 4

What Is the Relationship Between Syria and the World?

Chapter Preface

In August and September 2013, Syrian president Bashar al-Assad was accused of using chemical weapons against rebels. The United States wanted a United Nations resolution condemning the attacks and holding Assad responsible. But China consistently joined Russia on the UN Security Council in vetoing any UN action.

Why does China support Assad? There are a number of reasons. First, China and Syria are important trading partners. Since Assad visited China in 2004, trade has boomed. By 2008 China was Syria's biggest supplier of imported products.

More important than trade, however, is geopolitics. China is an authoritarian state. As such, it has been very concerned about the Arab Spring, a wave of revolutions and protests that has swept across the Middle East, unseating a number of dictatorial governments. The Syrian revolts are part of the Arab Spring, and the Chinese view them with suspicion. In addition, China is concerned about the chaos that might result if Syria collapses. China is particularly worried that a successful Sunni Muslim takeover in Syria may inspire protests by China's own Sunni population of ethnic Uighurs.

China also backs Assad in part because America does not. China is concerned about the growth of US power and is especially opposed to the unilateral use of US military force to overthrow regimes, no matter how noxious those regimes may be.

In 2009, China was persuaded to abstain from a UN vote to allow the United States to use force against Libya. The force was supposed to avert a humanitarian crisis, but ended up unseating Libyan dictator Muammar Qaddafi. China felt that it had been betrayed. According to Central Intelligence Agency analyst Christopher Johnson, China believes that if it does not "draw the line on Syria, then the next step is Iran, and then

Central Asia, and then [the Americans] are on [China's] back-door." In other words, China sees US interventions as destabilizing and potentially threatening. The leaders of China protect Assad not because they have any particular love for him but because they are predisposed to support the status quo.

The authors in this chapter debate Syria's international relations, focusing on the country's relationship with Iran, Great Britain, and Russia.

> "If the US does attack Syria ... that could tip the argument in favor of those in the Iranian leadership who want to distance themselves from Assad."

Iran May Cease Aiding Assad

Ariel Ben Solomon

Ariel Ben Solomon is Middle East correspondent for the Jerusalem Post. *In the following viewpoint, he reports that elements within the Iranian government, including former president and opposition leader Hashemi Rafsanjani, are pushing to end Iranian aid to Assad. In particular, Rafsanjani has asked that the Iranian government end recruitment aimed at staffing paramilitaries in Syria. The opposition leader was also reported to have accused Assad of using poison gas against his own people, according to Solomon.*

As you read, consider the following questions:

1. What is the al-Quds force, according to Solomon?

2. Who is Nooshabeh Amiri, according to the author?

3. How did ILNA's reporting of Rafsanjani's remarks about chemical attacks in Syria change, according to Solomon?

Events in Syria have reportedly prompted key Iranian figures to express their opposition to Tehran's ongoing involvement in helping Syrian President Bashar Assad remain in power.

Sources inside Iran claim that former president and opposition leader Hashemi Rafsanjani asked the commander of the Iranian al-Quds Brigades, Maj.-Gen. Qassem Suleimani, to stop sending volunteers to fight in Syria, according to a report published in the Iraqi daily *Azzaman*.

Rafsanjani asked Suleimani to stop the recruitment campaign using al-Quds Brigades' offices in Tehran and other Iranian cities, the report stated, adding that people were using emotional pleas or offers of money to convince recruits to fight in Syria. The article also claimed that the reason behind the campaign is that Iran fears the consequences of a possible US attack against Syria.

The sources said that there was a trend inside Iran that opposed interference in Syria and economic aid to the regime, especially considering the fact that the country was suffering under economic sanctions.

The al-Quds force is an elite unit of Iran's Revolutionary Guards Corps, which seeks to protect the regime.

In addition, the sources added that elements from the al-Quds Brigades and the Basij militia were roaming through the mosques and neighborhoods of Tehran and other cities in search of recruits to fight in Syria.

These efforts could increase if the US strikes Iran, said the sources, who claimed that thousands of Iranians had responded to the call.

The recruits are being trained under the supervision of the al-Quds Brigades before being sent to Syria via Iraq.

Meir Javedanfar, a lecturer on Iranian politics at the IDC [Interdisciplinary Center] in Herzliya, [Israel] told *The Jerusalem Post* that there were divisions among the top leadership in

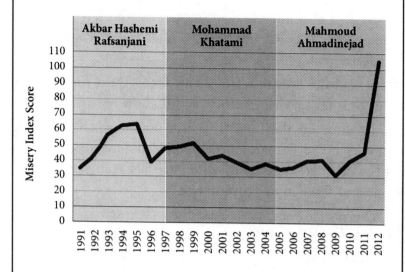

Iran Misery Index 1991–2012

Misery Index = Inflation Rate (End of Year) + Bank Lending Rates (Average of Manufacturing and Mining Rates) + Unemployment Rate − Annual Percent Change in Per Capita GDP.

Data from International Monetary Fund, www.eranico.com (accessed September 10, 2012), Economist Intelligence Unit, Central Bank of the Islamic Republic of Iran, and author's calculations.

TAKEN FROM: Steve H. Hanke, "Iran: Down, But Not Out," Cato Institute, October 2012. www.cato.org.

Iran with moderates led by [Iran President] Hassan Rouhani and Rafsanjani, who want to improve relations with the Saudis [US allies].

The People Want Peace

A change in direction is difficult to fathom if [Supreme leader of Iran and Shia cleric Ali] Khameini continues with his current policies on Syria, said Javedanfar.

"If the US does attack Syria, that means Assad is going to need a lot more money and weapons. And that eventually could tip the argument in favor of those in the Iranian leadership who want to distance themselves from Assad," he said.

The *Post* also interviewed Nooshabeh Amiri, a journalist based in Paris who left Iran in 2005 after being persecuted by the government.

She and her husband, Houshang Asadi, spent time in and out of prisons, surviving torture and the loss of their home.

An editor for the Iranian website Rooz, which is staffed mostly by exiled Iranian journalists and published in France, Amiri said there was a big difference between the Iranian people and those in the government.

"The people want peace and the extremists in power do not," she said, adding that there were politicians who believe that there should be more internal discussion about the country's involvement in Syria.

Rafsanjani and Assad's Poison Gas

Meanwhile, the Iranian Foreign Ministry denied comments attributed to Rafsanjani that accused the Syrian government of using poison gas in the country's civil war, saying the remarks had been "distorted."

The Iranian Labor News Agency (ILNA) quoted Rafsanjani as saying Syrian authorities had fired chemical weapons at their own people. Hours later, ILNA replaced the report with one that did not attribute blame for the attack.

"The statements of the chair of the Expediency Council [Rafsanjani] were distorted and have been denied by his office," said Marzieh Afkham, spokeswoman for the Iranian Foreign Ministry, according to the news agency.

ILNA initially quoted Rafsanjani as saying, "The people have been the target of a chemical attack by their own government and now they must also wait for an attack by foreigners."

In its subsequent report, he was quoted as saying, "On the one hand, the people of Syria are the target of a chemical attack, and now they must wait for an attack by foreigners."

A recording of Rafsanjani saying the original reported comments was posted online on September 2 [2013]. MEMRI (the Middle East Media Research Institute) provides a recording of him saying: "The Syrian people are experiencing harsh conditions. On the one hand, they are bombed with chemicals by their own government, and on the other hand, they can expect American bombs."

He also says that Iran is suffering from "real problems" and that the country is "besieged" by sanctions and a boycott. A greater danger may come, he says, if Syria is attacked.

Amiri mentioned that Rafsanjani's office had released a one-sentence statement published on his website seeking to clarify the controversy: "Neither chemical bombardment nor putting the people of Syria in danger has any political or humanistic justification."

The statement is general in nature and does not confirm or deny the content of Rafsanjani's original statement.

> "It will not make any difference if the dozens of missiles likely to soon be slamming Damascus won't be launched by Her Majesty's submarines. The U.S. Navy has enough Tomahawk cruise-missiles of its own."

The British Rejection of Military Action Will Have Little Effect on Syria

Anshel Pfeffer

Anshel Pfeffer is the Jewish World correspondent for the Jewish newspaper Haaretz. In the following viewpoint, he argues that the British Parliament vote against using military force in Syria will have little effect on Syria. He argues that the United States still has sufficient forces to bomb Syria in retaliation for chemical weapons attacks, and contends that the relationship between Britain and the United States should not be damaged by this vote. He adds that it is so far uncertain whether the Parliamentary decision will have an effect on the relationship between Israel and Britain.

As you read, consider the following questions:

1. How could British prime minister Cameron have won the vote with ease, in Pfeffer's opinion?

2. What strains does the author say the alliance between Britain and America has experienced in the past?

3. What does Pfeffer say was the unspoken allegation against Israel by Parliament members?

Syria's President Bashar Assad can smile this morning as he prepares his bunker somewhere deep beneath Damascus. But even he knows that [British prime minister] David Cameron's defeat overnight Friday [when the British Parliament voted against intervention in Syria] did not remove the threat looming over his head. To those on the receiving end, it will not make any difference if the dozens of missiles likely to soon be slamming Damascus, won't be launched by Her Majesty's submarines. The U.S. Navy has enough Tomahawk cruise-missiles of its own (the same ones the U.S. supplied Britain with anyway). The British prime minister's downfall is mainly an internal British matter.

A Lack of Confidence

During the long debate, no less than ninety-nine members of parliament [MPs] asked to speak; some supported, others had some objections (many of them justified) to Cameron's motion. But the operation against Assad, which was hastily put together and does not promise to diminish Syria's chemical arsenal nor make any long-term guarantees, was not the main reason for thirty members of the Conservative party to oppose Cameron's proposal.

He promised anyway to return to parliament for a second vote before the operation, they could have waited until then. Doubtless, for many of the MPs this was a way to expiate for the ostensible crime a decade earlier, when the parliament supported embarking on the Iraq war, a decision that was based on shoddy intelligence. However, the trauma of Iraq did not prevent them from voting against a much larger offensive against Libya two years ago [in 2011].

Since [the vote], historians have been trying to recall the last time the British parliament voted against a prime minister on matters of war and peace. Was it 1855 or 1780? Over the centuries, the house voted many times for unpopular and controversial wars. [Prime Minister] Tony Blair succeeded despite a massive public protest to pass the Iraq war through parliament and with a sizable majority at that.

[Prime Minister] Margaret Thatcher didn't even think she needed its authorization to send thousands of soldiers on a crazy adventure to reclaim the Falkland Islands in the southernmost reaches of the Atlantic (which despite the Pentagon's predictions, succeeded). [The] vote was not a confidence motion and Cameron doesn't have to resign, but it was above all a vote of no confidence in him as a leader and politician. He could have won the vote with relative ease if he had not been so high-handed with members of his party and the opposition (one of his aides accused Ed Miliband, leader of the opposition, for "giving succor to Assad").

The slim majority of 13 MPs against the Syrian operation could be the harbinger of a period of British isolationism, but it would be premature to divine national trends from one close vote. Parliament [after the vote] was not distancing itself from the world, it was simply saying it was not prepared to follow Cameron blindly into battle.

The Special Relationship Not Damaged

[The] vote will probably have very little effect on the wider issue of the future strike on Syria. The [Barack] Obama administration still seems resolved to prove the world the U.S. will not stand by while the Syrians are using chemical weapons. The attack will go forward, maybe even earlier than if Britain were taking part. Five American destroyers and an unknown number of submarines are more than enough for what will probably be a rather limited operation. And since for now only a one-off strike is planned, not all-out war, the issue of international consensus is less important. It will be interesting to see whether France now comes forward to take Britain's place—but either way it's not crucial.

Some British commentators were quick to bid farewell to the "special relations" between the U.S and the U.K. But the ties between the former empire and its colony ceased to be special when Barack Obama, a man with no sentiments for the Old World, entered the White House. Britain remains a major ally of the U.S., but it's not a senior partner or a first among equals. On the other hand, the cooperation between the two nations has been through much worse. Britain refused to take part in the Vietnam War and America remained out of World War Two, leaving Britain to fight Germany on its own for over two years until they were dragged in by [the Japanese attack on] Pearl Harbor. The Syrian Civil War is far from over and Britain may yet feel compelled to become involved.

Cameron's failure may also have repercussions for Jerusalem. Israel was barely mentioned in the long debate but it wasn't totally absent. Two veteran Israel-bashers tried to drag it in. [Respect Party MP] George Galloway, who refuses even to share a debating stage with Israelis, took his colleagues to task for not mentioning the occupation and settlements. [Labour Party MP] Gerald Kaufman mentioned "the use by Israel of illegal chemical weapons in Gaza"—he was referring to the phosphorus smoke-screen shells used by the IDF [Israel Defense Force] in Operation Cast Lead and was probably not aware that the British army also has similar NATO [North Atlantic Treaty Organization]-issue munitions. A few others seemed genuinely concerned for Israel's safety when they raised the fear that Assad could retaliate with more chemical attacks, this time against Israel. But before the debate, in a number of media interviews, there was also an atmosphere of suspicion towards Israel's motives in supplying intelligence which proved Syrian use of nerve gas. They may not have said it outright but there was an unspoken allegation that Israel may be pushing Britain to war.

But Israel's main concern will be for Britain's foreign policy from now on. The Cameron government, like its predecessors, is a central ally in the secret war against Iran. As a global finance center, London has been at the forefront of economic sanctions against the Islamic Republic. This led two years ago [in 2011] to the sacking of the British embassy in Tehran, and the suspension of diplomatic relations between the two nations. It's too early to predict whether Cameron's failure to leave his mark on the region will affect his outlook on Iran—it could even spur him to increase his support of sanctions. But the slap in the face from parliament and public opinion may have taken away all his appetite for foreign involvement.

"The British vote removes any plausible claim that the [Obama] Administration can assume consent—that the proper reaction to the horror in Syria is so obvious, so rooted in 'norms' that one needn't even ask."

The British Rejection of Military Action Should Have a Major Effect on the US Approach to Syria

Amy Davidson

Amy Davidson is a senior editor at the New Yorker *magazine. In the following viewpoint she asserts that David Cameron, the British prime minister, failed to address legitimate questions about the purpose and extent of the proposed military strike on Syria and that the British Parliament's rejection of his request for military force was a humiliating blow. She also says it should be a lesson to US president Barack Obama that he needs to consult Congress and should be prepared for tough questioning of, and possible rejection of, his argument for using military force against Syria.*

Amy Davidson, "The Cameron Trap: Obama's Lesson From the British Vote," *New Yorker*, August 30, 2013. © The New Yorker/Amy Davidson/Condé Nast.

As you read, consider the following questions:

1. According to Davidson, how was Cameron's defeat more than the Labour Party expected?

2. What bodies does Davidson say are not providing legal cover for US action in Iraq?

3. What does the author conclude is the "real Cameron trap"?

"It is clear to me that the British Parliament, reflecting the views of the British people, does not want to see British military action. I get that, and the government will act accordingly," Prime Minister David Cameron said, after he lost a vote meant to prepare the way for the bombing of Syria. He didn't say "I get that" with a politician's insinuating, put-on empathy, or as any sort of plea. The tone was sullen sarcasm: Fine, be that way.

Cameron Was Humiliated

The vote, 285-272, was unexpected, and a true political defeat for Cameron. It was more than even the opposition Labour Party had asked for—Ed Miliband, the opposition leader, had fought to get this vote and [a later] one, giving U.N. weapons inspectors time to gather evidence on [August 2013's] apparent chemical-weapons attack on civilians outside of Damascus. Now there won't be a second vote: Britain is done, Cameron is diminished, and President Obama should have reason to rethink what has been a haphazard rush to answer the horrible images from Syria with missiles. Here are some headlines in British papers [after the vote]:

CAMERON HUMILIATED AS MP'S VETO MISSLE STRIKE ON SYRIA (*Times of London*)

NO TO WAR, BLOW TO CAMERON (*Telegraph*)

THE HUMBLING OF CAMERON (*Sun*)

CAM DOWN (*Daily Mail*)

Humiliation is tied to pride. Parliament's anger had a great deal to do with process; . . . it took a small rebellion on the part of the public to remind the Prime Minister that he couldn't just rush off to war, shouting vague explanations over his shoulder as he went. Cameron's government had first approached Parliament with the sense that the decision had been made, that they were there just to approve, that there was no need to wait for the inspectors, just for the Prime Minister to get off the phone with Obama; in his speech to the House of Commons before the vote, Cameron said that he'd had to explain to Obama why he had even called them back at all. (He said he'd told the President that it was because of "the damage done to public confidence by Iraq.")

Worse, Cameron and his government suggested that asking hard questions about evidence, international law, and what exactly a military attack could accomplish—the sort of inquiry missing before Iraq—was a cowardly, morally inferior response to the horrible pictures from Syria, even a complicit one: "A lot of the arguments over this could give succor to the régime," a spokesman for Cameron said. That didn't go over well.

Congress Should Be Involved, Too

After the vote, American Secretary of Defense Chuck Hagel said that the White House didn't need Britain: it could act on its own, or maybe with France. But does alone also mean without Congress and the American public? That would be a mistake built on a mistake. (I've written so before.) Around the time that British Defense Secretary Philip Hammond—who probably didn't help matters by accidentally calling Assad "Saddam Hussein" on the BBC—was confirming that his country wouldn't be part of any military action, the Administration was holding a conference call with key members of Congress. That's not enough. According to a poll from NBC News, eighty per cent of Americans want Obama to get Congressional authorization before acting.

Cameron's failure in Parliament makes getting a vote from Congress more necessary—precisely *because* it might fail. The British vote removes any plausible claim that the Administration can assume consent—that the proper reaction to the horror in Syria is so obvious, so rooted in "norms" that one needn't even ask. The grounds in international law for military action are shaky, though. Neither the Arab League nor the [UN] Security Council are giving legal cover. Now there is not even an ersatz consensus of allies. That isn't to say that lone, noble stands are never right; but it should preclude a half-thought-out military action with little public support that dodges America's political processes and institutions.

Cameron, speaking to Parliament, said that bombing Syria wouldn't be about "taking sides," or "régime change," or "even about working more closely with the opposition"—just "our response to a war crime—nothing else." Neither he nor Obama has explained how to enforce that "nothing else" clause. What's the next step, when Assad reacts, and the next after that? Obama, if anything, was more vague in an interview on PBS:

> And if, in fact, we can take limited, tailored approaches, not getting drawn into a long conflict, not a repetition of, you know, Iraq, which I know a lot of people are worried about—but if we are saying in a clear and decisive but very limited way, we send a shot across the bow saying, stop doing this, that can have a positive impact on our national security over the long term, and may have a positive impact in the sense that chemical weapons are not used again on innocent civilians.

"Tailored approaches" seems to be the new "surgical strikes" (the worst euphemisms are those that involve bombs). As for that "shot across the bow"—where is it meant to land?

Answers Are Needed

Obama may take the British vote as proof that he can't risk putting himself in Cameron's position. But facing Congress after things don't go according to plan—if there even is a plan—would be all the more humiliating. Obama can't win this the way that Cameron lost it: by talking as though he is the only one acting according to principle, and that those who disagree just haven't seen enough pictures of the effects of chemical weapons. There are principles at work in wondering whether something that feels satisfying but causes more death and disorder is right, too. The real Cameron trap is thinking that a leader can go to war personally and apolitically, without having a good answer when asked what's supposed to happen after the missiles are fired. Does the President get that?

"*[Russia's abandoning of Assad will be]*
driven by [Syrian] opposition successes
on the ground, not by public pressure
from the Obama administration."

Russia Is Unlikely to Abandon Support for the Assad Regime Because of American Pressure

Dimitri Simes, as told to Bernard Gwertzman

Dimitri Simes is president and chief executive officer of the Center for the National Interest, and Bernard Gwertzman is a former New York Times *editor, now consulting editor for the website of the Council on Foreign Relations. In the following viewpoint, Simes tells Gwertzman that Russia's support for Syria is based on support for the principle of sovereignty and on mistrust of American motives. Simes says that Russia may abandon Assad if it is clear that his regime is about to fall, but it is unlikely to support military intervention. Simes concludes that American diplomacy with Russia has been high-handed and is unlikely to change the Russian position on Syria.*

As you read, consider the following questions:

1. How do weapons sales influence the Russian position on Syria, according to Simes?

Dimitri Simes interviewed by Bernard Gwertzman, "Why Russia Won't Yield on Syria," Council on Foreign Relations, July 17, 2012. Copyright © 2012 by Council on Foreign Relations. All rights reserved. Reproduced by permission.

2. Why does Simes say that US-Russian relations have deteriorated since September 11, 2001?

3. What impression does US support for opposition groups in Russia create, according to Simes?

UN Special Envoy to Syria Kofi Annan is in Moscow for talks with [Russian] President Vladimir Putin aimed at intensifying pressure on the Syrian regime through UN Security Council sanctions, but Russia expert Dimitri Simes says that while Russia might at some point get fed up with Bashar al-Assad and see that his government is losing ground, it isn't "as opposed to the Damascus regime as is the [Barack] Obama administration and many other governments." Putin is generally committed to "maintaining the sovereignty of existing states," especially since "most of the regimes that were changed after the Cold War [political tension between the West and the USSR and its allies, 1947–1991] were the regimes that were friendly to Russia," says Simes. Additionally, says Simes, Putin "is more skeptical of U.S. and Western intentions, particularly U.S. intentions," than former president [Dmitry] Medvedev, who had forged a good relationship with President Obama.

Humanitarianism vs. Sovereignty

[Bernard Gwertzman:] *Russian Foreign Minister Sergey Lavrov has indicated that Russia is not going to change its position about sanctions. Why is Moscow so supportive of the regime of Bashar al-Assad?*

[Dimitri Simes:] I don't think they're that supportive of the Damascus regime. A better way to put it is that they're not as opposed to the Damascus regime as the Obama administration and many other governments. Clearly, Russia has a rather different view of Assad. I don't think you can say Assad is a Moscow client. He certainly was not taking guidance from Moscow. He also for a number of months has stopped paying his bills, so he's not a reliable customer. He also is an embarrassment in terms of Russian relations, not only with the United States, but with most Arab countries and with Israel, a country economically more important to Russia than Syria.

Then explain Moscow's resistance to taking more concerted action against Syria.

The Putin government is opposed to the concept of regime change because Russia has a more traditional view of international law. Their emphasis is not on humanitarian principles, but on maintaining the sovereignty of existing states. After the end of the Cold War, most of the regimes that were changed were regimes that were friendly to Russia, whether you're talking about the Balkans, with the ouster of President Slobodan Milošević in Yugoslavia [unseated in part with US aid in 2000], or whether you're talking more recently about Libya [where Muammar al-Qaddafi was forced out of power with American help in 2011].

How much is the loyalty to Assad due to weapons sales? . . .

Assad is not in a position to buy new Russian weapons, but Russia has legal obligations under old contracts. It's already difficult for Russia to sell weapons abroad because their weapons are considered of inferior quality, certainly less reliable than those made in the West. One reason the Russians are still able to sell their weapons internationally is that they sell their weapons to governments that are not popular in the United States and NATO [North Atlantic Treaty Organization, a US–western European alliance]. If Russians are viewed as totally unreliable by such governments, their whole arms trade may go down the drain, and this is an important source of their income.

U.S.-Russian Mistrust

Russia and China abstained a year ago [2011] when the [UN] Security Council passed a resolution for a no-fly zone that al-

lowed NATO military force to be used against Muammar al-Qaddafi's forces. Does Putin, who was then prime minister and is now president, regret not vetoing the resolution?

I was in Moscow when this resolution was passed, and I talked to a senior foreign minister official who told me that they could not vote for the resolution as drafted. He supported the resolution's intent, but said the resolution required a lot of work because of too many ambiguities that could be interpreted by the United States and NATO in a more far-reaching way than Russia was comfortable with.

The next day, I went back to the ministry. By that time Russia had already abstained on the resolution. I bumped into the official I saw the day before, and he looked at me and smiled. He said, "Our president has his way of making decisions." Then I talked to people who were more representative of Putin's thinking, and they were quite flabbergasted. They said that this was Medvedev's decision, that President Obama talked to President Medvedev and proved to be very persuasive with him. They felt Medvedev was too deferential, and they predicted the United States would not be satisfied with the kind of conservative interpretation of a no-fly zone, and that it would inevitably lead to a NATO aerial assault. They were proven right. The Libya episode energized the Putin camp, and gave them evidence that Medvedev could not be trusted to stay as president and to run Russian national security.

How would you describe U.S.-Russian relations right now?

Putin was one of the first who called President George Bush after September 11 and offered his support. So it was not as if Putin had started as a dedicated opponent of the United States. But then his relationship with the Bush administration went downhill. President Putin, as did many in Russia, came to the conviction that Russia was not treated sufficiently as a great

Russia and September 11

Because of the war in Chechnya and the resulting wave of terrorist attacks in Russian cities, Moscow had focused on terrorism, especially Islamic terrorism, as the most immediate security challenge facing the country long before September 11, 2001. Until 9/11, the United States routinely condemned what it termed Russia's use of excessive force in waging what was essentially a counterinsurgency campaign in Chechnya—while Moscow responded that Washington lacked a proper frame of reference because it did not face the terrorist threat directly. With the attacks in New York and Washington, Islamic terrorism suddenly became the top security threat for the United States as well. To many Russians, September 11 had proven that Moscow had been right about terrorism all along and that now the United States would come to see the problem in the same light.

Jeffrey Mankoff,
Russian Foreign Policy, 2012.

power by the United States, and that the United States was more committed to changes around Russia, [such as] bringing former Soviet republics and allies into NATO or the European Union, than in having a constructive relationship with Russia.

Despite the "reset" under President Obama and President Medvedev, many people around Putin were not persuaded there was a qualitative change in the U.S.-Russian relationship. The bottom line is that Putin is more hard-nosed; he is more skeptical of U.S. and Western intentions, particularly U.S. intentions, and he's not personally mesmerized by President Obama the way Medvedev was.

Shaming Russia

Russia has proposed extending the UN observer mission in Syria, which is due to expire on July 20 [2012] unless it's extended. Lavrov suggested that the Western countries are trying to blackmail Russia by saying that they would not vote for an extension of the observer mission if Russia did not support the resolution to put more sanctions on Syria.

Shaming Russia publicly, the way Secretary Hillary Clinton has done on several occasions, [is] unlikely to work on Putin and only toughens his stand. What may change the Russian perspective is what is happening inside Syria. If you look at Russian TV coverage of Syria, it is quite clear that they're now hedging their bets, that they understand Assad is losing ground; they're reporting recent prominent defections from Assad's inner circle.

At a certain point, Russians may say to themselves that the game is all over in Syria, or at least almost over. They would not want to be the last ones to be committed to this man who is not viewed in Moscow as the same kind of villain he's viewed as in Washington, but he's not quite a hero either. At some point they may decide to give up on him and to start looking for bringing about regime change. They're not quite there yet. Movement in that direction is driven by opposition successes on the ground, not by public pressure from the Obama administration. Also, Russians think the Obama administration is a little hypocritical, because as they have told Washington, [if] it is so committed to removing Assad, they certainly can do it the way it was done in Iraq, the way it was done during the liberation of Kosovo from Serbia, without Security Council blessing. The Russians are saying it would be a mistake, they would criticize it, but they would not resist it militarily, and it would not be a defining issue in the Russian-American relationship. Russian officials believe the Obama administration really does not want to intervene in Syria, but they're using Russia as a whipping boy, to blame on Russia what the Obama administration does not quite want to do itself.

What does Washington say?

The administration acts under the assumption that they can have their cake and eat it too in relations with anyone in the world, including proud powers such as China and Russia. Secretary Clinton, for instance, while she's trying to persuade the Russians to support a tough Syrian resolution, at the same time went to St. Petersburg and organized a meeting with opposition activists and promised that the United States would find some creative way to support Russian opposition groups despite new legislation passed by the Russian Duma [lower house of the Russian legislature], which requires such groups, if they accept foreign money and engage in political activity, to be registered as foreign agents. Do I like this legislation passed by the Russian Duma? Absolutely not. This legislation is counterproductive for Russia and will be a problem in the U.S.-Russian relationship. But at the same time, if Syria is such a central problem for the United States, wouldn't it be wise for the secretary of state on this particular trip to Russia not to meet with opposition activists? Because it creates an impression in Moscow that the only reason the United States is not calling for an end to the Putin government is because Russia is a major nuclear power. That impression certainly does not make Russia more forthcoming on issues of concern to the United States.

> *"If [Syrian president Bashar al-Assad's] prospects dim—as seems likely—some minor rephrasing of the U.N. resolution will likely be enough to satisfy Russian concerns and bring them on board."*

Why Russia Protects Syria's Assad

Daniel Treisman

Daniel Treisman is a professor in the Department of Political Science at the University of California–Los Angeles (UCLA) and the author of The Return: Russia's Journey from Gorbachev to Medvedev. *In the following viewpoint, Treisman argues that Russian support of Bashar al-Assad is merely pragmatic. Russia has military and commercial links with the Syrian regime. Moreover, it is unimpressed with Western moral arguments, since Washington has stood on the sidelines while other dictators, such as those in Uzbekistan and Bahrain, crush resistance. Treisman concludes that if Assad looks like he is about to lose, Russia may abandon him, again for pragmatic rather than moral reasons.*

As you read, consider the following questions:

1. What Russian strategic interests are at stake in Tartus, Syria, according to Treisman?

2. Why is Uzbekistan important to the West, in the author's opinion?

3. For Russia, Treisman says, what is the Syrian civil war about, if it is not a struggle between a people and a dictator?

As casualties mount before the brutal onslaught of Bashar al-Assad's forces against Syria's pro-democracy protesters, the Russians are being unhelpful again. In Washington and Brussels [Belgium], even habitually cool diplomats have been showing frustration.

On January 31 [2012] Russia joined with China to block a plan presented to the U.N. Security Council by Morocco and supported by the Arab League that called on Assad to hand power to his deputy, who would then call a general election. If Assad did not comply within 15 days, the resolution threatened undisclosed "further measures."

Moscow already had vetoed one resolution denouncing Assad's use of force in October [2011]. As Western leaders sought to pry the Syrian dictator from power, his old friends in Moscow sent an aircraft-carrying missile cruiser to Syrian waters in a show of support last month and shipped his troops a consignment of Yakhont cruise missiles.

Such actions are just the latest in a litany of obstructionist maneuvers and spoiler ploys whose goal often appears merely to undermine Western international objectives. From Washington, Moscow has seemed determined to soften or delay sanctions on Iran aimed at curbing its nuclear ambitions, to stall in talks with North Korea over its nuclear weapons, to intimidate pro-democracy movements in neighboring states, and to egg on anti-American dictators such as [Venezuela's] Hugo Chavez.

Western commentators typically attribute such behavior to Putin's personal paranoia or to attempts to rekindle the nation's wounded pride and assert Russia's superpower status. Look a little closer, however, and Russia's actions seem motivated more by calculated—albeit sometimes miscalculated—realpolitik than by psychological impulses.

First, strategic interests are at stake. Tartus, Syria hosts the sole remaining Russian naval base on the Mediterranean, currently being refurbished by 600 Russian technicians after long disuse. To have to give up this Middle Eastern beachhead would be a shame, as far as the Russians are concerned.

Second, although limited, Russia has real commercial interests in Syria. Contracts to sell arms to Damascus—both those signed and under negotiation—total $5 billion. Having lost $13 billion due to international sanctions on Iran and $4.5 billion in canceled contracts to Libya, Russia's defense industry is already reeling. Besides arms exports, Russian companies have major investments in Syria's infrastructure, energy and tourism sectors, worth $19.4 billion in 2009.

Counting pennies while protesters are gunned down may seem cynical. "How many people need to die before the consciences of world capitals are stirred?" Britain's Foreign Secretary William Hague demanded on January 31, [2012,] clearly thinking of Moscow.

Western Double Standards

But Russian policymakers have developed an allergy to Western leaders' moralizing. Just as it was pressing al-Assad to resign, the U.S. State Department quietly lifted a ban on military aid to the [Islamic] Karimov dictatorship in Uzbekistan, which had butchered its own protesters a few years earlier. (Uzbekistan is important for supply lines to NATO troops in Afghanistan.) Neither did Washington press the king of Bahrain—where the U.S. Navy has a port—to step down after he crushed popular demonstrations in his capital.

Repression in Bahrain

The human rights situation in Bahrain has markedly deteriorated over recent months, with repressive practices increasingly entrenched and more and more flagrant government disregard for the recommendations of the Bahrain Independent Commission of Inquiry (BICI), set up to investigate widespread human rights violations during the 2011 uprising. The blanket ban issued in late October 2012 on all protests, and the increasing harassment and arrest of human rights activists, has meant [that] hope for an improved human rights situation in Bahrain is fading. . . .

The US and UK governments applauded the establishment of the BICI and welcomed its final report. Yet, in the face of the worsening human rights situation in the country, Bahrain's two allies have been more vocal in their criticism of the country's human rights record.

However, officials have not matched these expressions of concern with any meaningful actions or consequences. Indeed, both governments continue to call for reconciliation and reform in Bahrain, clinging to the illusion of reform and minimizing blows to the stated reform process.

Amnesty International, Bahrain:
Reform Shelved, Repression Unleashed, *2012.*

From Washington, the West's recent interventions in the Middle East seem unplanned and responsive, with modest goals. From Moscow, it is easy to see a pattern in the repeated use of force to overthrow leaders—from Afghanistan and Iraq to Libya—and diplomatic pressure to dislodge others—in Tunisia, Egypt and Yemen. President George W. Bush may be gone, but his "Freedom Agenda," it sometimes seems, lives on.

Libya is a particularly sore point. Russia's leaders felt they were tricked into supporting a resolution to protect civilians only to see it used to provide cover for airstrikes to overthrow Moammar Gadhafi. Vague phrases like "further measures" now set off alarm bells.

Beyond commercial and strategic interests, the Kremlin's [that is, the Russian government's] greatest fear is of instability in the Middle East and Central Asia. Russian policymakers already worry about the northward spread of Islamic militancy and opium if the departure of NATO from Afghanistan leads to Taliban resurgence and state collapse.

Rather than a fairytale struggle between the people and a dictator, they see a potentially explosive religious conflict between Syria's ruling Alawis (close to Shi'a Islam) and majority Sunnis. The zeal with which rulers of the Gulf states and some in Washington call for al-Assad's ouster seems part of a broader project to isolate Iran, Syria's ally.

Still, unless al-Assad manages to decisively defeat his opposition in short order, the Russians are likely to soften their position—not because of moral arguments, but simply because they do not want to end up on the losing side. If they alienate al-Assad's successors, the very interests they seek to protect could be in jeopardy. Russian Foreign Secretary Sergei Lavrov hinted at a shift on January 31 [2012], saying: "We are not friends or allies of President Assad."

Picking the perfect moment to dump a congenial dictator is never easy—consider Washington's contortions over Hosni Mubarak in Egypt and the French embarrassment over their late coddling of Gadhafi. Walking out too soon risks alarming other allies. Waiting too long creates the image that one is both reactionary and out of touch.

The Kremlin's policymakers are hardly adept at this, and certainly may wait too long. So far, they believe al-Assad still has a reasonable chance of survival. If his prospects dim—as seems likely—some minor rephrasing of the U.N. resolution will likely be enough to satisfy Russian concerns and bring them on board.

| "This diplomatic turn looks like doing little to punish Syria's use of chemical weapons . . . [but] it may be the least bad option."

Using Russian Diplomacy to Strip Syria of Chemical Weapons May Be the Least Bad Option

The Economist

The Economist *is a well-known and respected British news publication. It reports in the following viewpoint on Russia's proposal to avert a military strike on Syria by asking Assad to turn over all of his chemical weapons. The Economist *says that the United States has seized on the plan to stall for time since other diplomatic efforts have been stalled largely by the unpopularity of proposed air strikes with the United States and international public. The viewpoint concludes that Russia's proposal probably will not work but that this may be the best current option in the absence of a consensus for any other action.*

As you read, consider the following questions:

1. According to *The Economist,* why did US actions in Libya lead Russia to oppose action in Syria?

2. What does the author say will be the first challenge to any system of inspection?

3. According to the author, how could Obama have used his address to the nation to increase control over the diplomatic process?

"**A**merica is not the world's policeman—terrible things happen across the globe, and it is beyond our means to right every wrong". That world-weary run-up to his conclusion was about the clearest moment in President Barack Obama's televised address on Syria on September 10th [2013]. It was a speech that twisted and turned and contradicted itself, reflecting an astonishing fortnight [two-week period] which left Mr Obama looking like a spectator of his own foreign policy. First he put the onus of resolving the Syria crisis on an unwilling, risk-averse Congress, then on the government of Russia—just a day after his national security adviser, Susan Rice, had accused Russia of opposing "every form of accountability in Syria".

His address was a confounding use of the presidential bully pulpit. With patience, eloquence and passion, Mr Obama set out his judgment, as commander-in-chief, that launching targeted missile strikes in response to the use of chemical weapons by [Syrian president] Bashar Assad's regime was "in the national security interests of the United States". The president went on to make a moral case for action. Lest war-weary voters reject his course, though, he promised that he "would not put boots on the ground" and that his attack, while more than a "pinprick", would involve only "modest effort and risk".

Thus, in the words of Kenneth Pollack of the Brookings Institution, 90% of the address sounded like "the speech that the president would give to explain why he was using force—or had just done so". But having argued that action could not be safely or morally avoided, Mr Obama went on to say that he saw no "direct and imminent threat" to American security in Syria, and so had felt it right to seek congressional backing. And then, in the bombshell of the night, he announced that he was asking Congress to postpone any votes at all, to allow time for Russia to work on a diplomatic plan for Syria to give up its chemical weapons.

The Dealing's Done

It was too early to know if that diplomatic initiative could succeed, Mr Obama admitted. But—all talk of deterring others from imitating Syria apparently forgotten—he went on to say that "this initiative has the potential to remove the threat of chemical weapons without the use of force".

The contradictions swirling round Mr Obama could yet be resolved into a diplomatic triumph. In this remarkably optimistic scenario, Russia would make good on its unexpected offer to prod its ally, Mr Assad, to hand over all his stocks of chemical weapons to international control: a process helped along by a credible threat of American air strikes.

But such starry-eyed optimism hardly accounts for Mr Obama's ceding of the cat seat. Over the days running up to the speech it had become clear that a resolution giving Mr Obama broad authority to launch missiles against Syria would struggle to pass the Democrat-controlled Senate, let alone the Republican-controlled House of Representatives, where it would be opposed by liberal Democrats, libertarian Republicans and conservatives who simply do not trust Mr Obama on anything. Faced with defeat, even a probably unworkable and possibly insincere proposal from Russia seemed worth grabbing.

The proposal apparently came as a complete surprise. On September 9th John Kerry, America's secretary of state, answering a reporter's question about how, if at all, Syria could avert a strike, replied by saying that it could hand over all its chemical weapons forthwith.

Having previously called Mr Kerry a liar for denying the links between the Syrian opposition and al-Qaeda, Vladimir Putin, Russia's president, jumped on his seemingly off-the-cuff remark. As he showed with a remarkable appeal to international law and multilateralism in the *New York Times* on September 12th, Mr Putin is keen to be seen as a legitimate and indispensable player in world affairs. So at his boss's bidding Mr Kerry's Russian counterpart, Sergei Lavrov, took the opportunity to call on the Syrian regime to give up its stockpiles of chemical weapons and join the Chemical Weapons Convention (CWC), which bans their possession.

None of this was as impromptu as it seemed. In 2012, when Russia pulled out of a programme set up 20 years ago to help the former Soviet Union get rid of weapons of mass destruction, Richard Lugar, who as a senator had been one of the creators of the programme, suggested that the two countries could impose control over Syrian chemical weapons. The Russians buried the idea, arguing that the Syrian government needed no oversight. But it resurfaced last May when Mr Kerry brought it up on a visit to Moscow. It was fleshed out at a one-on-one meeting between Mr Obama and Mr Putin at the G20 [economic] summit in St Petersburg, Russia.

Russia has blocked every single attempt to impose sanctions against Syria. This, it has argued, has not been out of simple spite. Nor has it been because of a special cosiness with Mr Assad—who, as Mr Putin snarkily quipped, "spent more time in Paris than he did in Moscow". According to Dmitri Trenin, the head of the Carnegie Moscow Centre, a foreign-relations think-tank, in 2012 the Kremlin told America it would agree to the eventual removal of Mr Assad as part of a political transition to a secular government that would accommodate Russia's interests.

The recalcitrance boils down to Russia resenting the very idea of military pressure for regime change—or any action at all—without a resolution of the United Nations' Security Council, where it has a veto. Russia had felt duped when, in

2011, America, France and Britain bombed Libya to protect civilian lives. The bombing was thorough enough to topple the regime, and stretched the Security Council resolution which permitted it to the limit of its meaning; the image of Muammar Qaddafi's barbaric death stuck in Mr Putin's mind. Everything he has done since then has been to stave off military action by the West. The chemical-weapons plan is part of that effort.

Fyodor Lukyanov, editor of *Russia in Global Affairs*, argues that Russia's plan is not meant to be a confrontational anti-American gesture, but a way of restoring the countries' relationship. It hinges on the (correct) assumption that Mr Obama never wanted to go to war in Syria. By offering him a face-saving way out, Moscow thinks that it is doing him a favour, hoping to make him feel grateful and indebted. But Mr Obama knows that Russia cares more about the process than the result.

On the night of September 9th [2013], after the Russians made their intervention, France hastily put together a tough proposal for a Security Council resolution on Syria. It was to be tabled under Chapter Seven of the UN charter, authorising the use of force if Syria failed to comply, and called for dismantling of all Syria's chemical-weapons stocks, as well as the prosecution at the International Criminal Court of members of the regime responsible for the attacks.

François Hollande, the president of France, is keen to keep his country at the diplomatic fore over Syria. When he announced in late August that France would participate in military action to punish Mr Assad, he found himself in the unaccustomed position of having France lauded by Mr Kerry as America's oldest ally. But Mr Hollande was rather left in the lurch when Mr Obama decided to seek authorisation from Congress for military strikes. As Laurent Fabius, the French foreign minister, stressed when he announced the resolution: "We decided to take the initiative".

The Best That You Can Hope For

The new diplomatic push was also a way for Mr Hollande to deal with sceptical public opinion over Syria. Polls consistently show a majority of the French—like majorities of Britons and Americans—to be against military strikes. The French are particularly opposed to any action that lacks UN backing. They have not forgotten that the ill-fated American-led invasion of Iraq had no UN mandate because of a French threat to veto a resolution.

The risk for Mr Hollande is that he ends up looking naive. Mr Fabius said he was fully aware of the danger that the Russian proposal was a "diversionary tactic", but that it was worth testing Russia's word with a credible, binding resolution. Russia rejected France's plan for a Security Council resolution the same day because it invoked Chapter Seven, and because it blamed Syria for the attacks in the first place (which Russia, despite calling for disarmament, has not done). Even so, Mr Hollande is grateful for the diplomatic turn.

So is David Cameron. Britain's prime minister became embarrassingly irrelevant to the anti-Assad cause last month, after Parliament voted to forbid him to commit troops to it. A shift away from military action puts Britain back in the picture. With Russia apparently committed to reject anything that looks like an ultimatum, Britain is working with America on the Security Council resolution. Mr Cameron may even be congratulating himself on having played a role with Mr Putin—who is said to be more at ease with Mr Cameron, another self-confident cold-water swimmer, than with any other Western leader.

Time Enough for Counting

Plenty of diplomacy is yet to come. Mr Kerry and Mr Lavrov are set to meet in Geneva [Switzerland] on September 12th [2013]. If a UN inspection mission can be put together at all, it will take months, probably years. Small wonder the beleaguered Assad regime, well versed in obfuscation and diplomatic delay, welcomed the prospect with barely disguised glee. Syria's battered, fragmented and frustrated opposition bitterly resigned itself to doing without outside attacks. Its trajectory towards increased radicalism has steepened with the pervasive doubt that Mr Assad will be promptly punished for gassing his people.

The first challenge for any system of inspection will be finding stuff to inspect. One source familiar with American assessments says that if they knew 90–95% of the places where the weapons were before the fog of civil war descended over the country, they may now know only 50%. The only way an inspection regime would be able to get all of the chemical weapons, which can be outwardly indistinguishable from other munitions, would be if the regime was fully co-operative. If it is not, finding the weapons and the chemicals they are made from would be impossible.

Co-operation could conceivably have benefits for the Syrian regime beyond just deflecting air strikes. The process of consolidating the weapons at a few facilities might have tactical benefits, allowing the army to abandon isolated weapons facilities it must now protect and to concentrate forces where they are needed for fighting. If the inspectors felt they had full co-operation, they might not have to ask too many questions about the sources of the weapons and the technology that went into them. The answers to such questions might embarrass some of Syria's friends.

Even if the Syrians were to co-operate, though, keeping hundreds of inspectors safe would be incredibly taxing; attempts to do so would require tens of thousands of soldiers even in a "semi-permissive" environment. Where they might come from, when America's president is committed to putting no boots on the ground, is a mystery. So experts judge that a hard ceasefire is a necessity for any serious inspections. And it would have to last a long time.

Syria's stocks of chemical weaponry are large: French intelligence estimates talk of tens of tonnes of VX, the most lethal nerve agent, and hundreds of tonnes of both sarin, another nerve agent, and mustard gas. It may be that all the nerve agents are in "binary" systems, which work by mixing much safer chemicals together to form toxins only at the moment the weapon is used. Such weapons are safer to transport than those which are deadly from their creation, so it might be possible to move them out of the country, if there are borders which are peaceful enough to allow it and if a country with the wherewithal to dispose of the stuff is ready to take them in. But even if all the nerve agents could be removed, it seems likely that the mustard gas would have to be disposed of more or less where it is. That would require purposely-built facilities inside Syria.

It would all be very costly and dauntingly, dangerously slow. Under the CWC, Japan is required to deal with chemical weapons it left in China after the second world war. The process has been going on since 1999 and is expected to cost perhaps $9 billion. And that is a smaller task, undertaken a long way from any war zone. Elsewhere, people are still working on destroying weapons made before their use was banned under the 1925 Geneva protocol: "Last time I visited Porton Down," says an American of Britain's chemical-weapons centre, "they were working on destroying things from the first world war".

Learn to Play It Right

And what of the credibility of Mr Obama's threat to strike if Mr Assad does not co-operate? Congress remains skittish and deeply wary of sharing the responsibility for unpopular military strikes. In his televised address, Mr Obama asked his "friends on the right" to reconcile their commitment to America's military might with a failure to act in a clearly just cause. Addressing anti-war Democrats—some of whom have reported anger from constituents at the idea of spending any more money on foreign adventures—Mr Obama asked his "friends on the left" to realise that when Syrian children have been filmed writhing in pain on a cold hospital floor, resolutions and condemnations are not enough. Talk of a diplomatic track may move some of those friends, but not all.

Mr Obama did not have to go to Congress for permission to strike Syria: he chose to do so, shocking many of his own aides, for essentially domestic political reasons. Mr Obama's opponents in Congress were uniting behind a charge that he was flouting the constitution in declining to consult them. If he had gone ahead alone with an unpopular action, Republicans seemed certain to snipe from the sidelines. Thus he decided to force Congress to take a stand. Alas, he misjudged his ability to shift the public mood. On September 10th, [2013,] before his speech, he conceded to Senate Republicans that "I'm good, but not that good", according to Senator Mark Kirk, a Republican who backs military action.

The president could have used his televised address to increase his control over the uncertain, Russian-led diplomatic track by spelling out what, by when, would constitute a satisfactory Syrian response. He could have asked Congress to pass a new resolution supporting his timetable and demands, and backing it with a credible threat of force. But he merely told Congress to postpone any votes to authorise force "while we pursue this diplomatic path", before reaffirming, in closing, that through this diplomacy and, if necessary, force, America could still do some good.

So Mr Obama has been left sounding like a commentator on his own policy. By seeming to slow any hint of a rush to war, the diplomatic gambit may make it easier to get some sort of motion through the Senate. A bipartisan group of senators is putting together something along those lines. In the long run, though, this diplomatic turn looks like doing little to punish Syria's use of chemical weapons—it can only succeed if Mr Assad acquiesces in forsaking them—and hardly looks like a deterrent to anyone elsewhere wanting to build a stockpile. It may be the least bad option. That doesn't make it a cause for hope.

Periodical and Internet Sources Bibliography

The following articles have been selected to supplement the diverse views presented in this chapter.

Geneive Abdo	"What an Attack on Syria Will Mean for US-Iran Relations," *Al Jazeera*, September 10, 2013. www.aljazeera.com.
Julian Borger	"UK Pledges Further £100m Relief to Syria," *The Guardian* (Manchester, UK), September 25, 2013.
Jeremy Bowen	"Syria Hails US-Russia Deal on Chemical Weapons," *BBC News*, September 15, 2013. www.bbc.co.uk.
CBS News	"U.S., Russia in First Talks Since Syria Deal," October 6, 2013. www.cbsnews.com.
Robert Fisk	"Iran to Send 4,000 Troops to Aid President Assad's Forces in Syria," *Independent* (London), June 16, 2013.
Conor Friedersdorf	"The Vote Against War in the U.K.: No David Cameron Hasn't Been Humiliated," *The Atlantic*, August 30, 2013.
National Public Radio	"Examining Britain's Position on the Crisis in Syria," September 25, 2013. www.npr.org.
Jason Rezaian	"In Iran, a Change in Tone on Syria," *Washington Post*, September 4, 2013.
Reuters	"US Opens Door to Iran Taking Part in Syria Peace Conference," *Jerusalem Post*, October 7, 2013.
Israel Shamir	"Russia, Syria and the Decline of American Hegemony," *CounterPunch*, October 8, 2013.

For Further Discussion

Chapter 1

1. None of the viewpoints make a case for a full-scale land invasion of Syria. On the basis of the evidence presented in this chapter, should the United States invade Syria with an army and overthrow Assad? Why or why not? Cite from the viewpoints in your answer.

2. Should a US president be able to use military force without approval from Congress? Why or why not?

Chapter 2

1. Should the United States be willing to fund moderate Islamic groups in the Syrian resistance? Why or why not? Explain your answer using evidence from this and the previous chapter.

2. Would there be any advantages of a protracted war in Syria in which neither side wins (think Iraq)? Any disadvantages? Explain your answer.

Chapter 3

1. On the basis of the information in this chapter, do you think the United States should work to move significant numbers of Syrian refugees to the United States? Why or why not?

2. Are there ever legitimate reasons to refuse refugees? Explain your answer using examples from this chapter.

Chapter 4

1. Iran is an Islamic regime; Syria, though a Muslim country, has a secular government. Why does Iran nonetheless support Assad?

2. Is Russia supporting Assad simply because the United States opposes him? Why or why not?

Organizations to Contact

The editors have compiled the following list of organizations concerned with the issues debated in this book. The descriptions are derived from materials provided by the organizations. All have publications or information available for interested readers. The list was compiled on the date of publication of the present volume; names, addresses, phone and fax numbers, and e-mail and Internet addresses may change. Be aware that many organizations take several weeks or longer to respond to inquiries, so allow as much time as possible.

The Brookings Institution

1775 Massachusetts Ave. NW, Washington, DC   20036-2188
(202) 797-6000
e-mail: communications@brookings.edu
website: www.brookings.edu

The institution, founded in 1927, is a liberal think tank that conducts research and education in foreign policy, economics, government, and the social sciences. It publishes numerous books and the quarterly *Brookings Review*. Its website includes numerous papers and articles, including "Syria's Unseen Crisis: Displaced Women Face Rape, Insecurity, Poverty," and "Weighing U.S. Intervention: Syria v. Congo."

Cato Institute

1000 Massachusetts Ave. NW, Washington, DC   20001-5403
(202) 842-0200 • fax: (202) 842-3490
website: www.cato.org

The institute is a libertarian public policy research foundation dedicated to increasing the understanding of public policies from the perspective of principles of limited government, free markets, individual liberty, and peace. It publishes the *Cato Journal* three times a year, the *Cato Policy Analysis* periodically, and *Cato Policy Review*, a bimonthly newsletter. Its website also includes articles such as "Don't Arm Syria's Rebels," and "Intervention in Libya and Syria Isn't Humanitarian Or Liberal."

Center for Middle Eastern Studies
University of Texas, Austin, TX 78712
(512) 471-3881 • fax: (512) 471-7834
e-mail: cmes@menic.utexas.edu
website: www.utexas.edu/cola/depts/mes

The center was established by the US Department of Education to promote a better understanding of the Middle East. It provides research and instructional materials and publishes a number of scholarly and literary publication series, including The Emerging Voices from the Middle East Series, the Binah Yitzrit Foundation Series in Israel Studies, the Middle East Monograph Series, the Modern Middle East Series, and the Middle Eastern Languages in Translation Series.

Council on Foreign Relations
58 E. Sixty-Eighth St., New York, NY 10021
(212) 434-9400 • fax: (212) 434-9800
e-mail: communications@cfr.org
website: www.cfr.org

The council researches the international aspects of American economic and political policies. Its journal *Foreign Affairs*, published five times a year, provides analysis on global conflicts. Articles on its website include "Syria's Continuing Civil War," and "The Hezbollah Connection in Syria and Iran."

Human Rights Watch (HRW)
350 Fifth Ave., 34th Fl., New York, NY 10118-3299
(212) 290-4700 • fax: (212) 736-1300
e-mail: hrwnyc@hrw.org
website: www.hrw.org

HRW is an international organization dedicated to ensuring that the human rights of individuals worldwide are observed and protected. In order to achieve this protection, HRW investigates allegations of human rights abuses then works to hold violators, be they governments or individuals, accountable for their actions. The organization's website is divided by continent, offering specific information on individual countries and issues. It includes numerous reports on human rights in Syria.

International Institute for Strategic Studies (IISS)

1850 K St. NW, Ste. 300, Washington, DC 20006
(202) 659-1490 • fax: (202) 296-1134
website: www.iiss.org

The IISS is a leading world authority on political-military conflict. It has an international membership and focuses on researching and distributing information about international strategic issues. Its publications include *The Military Balance*, an annual assessment of 170 countries' defense capabilities, and *Survival: Global Politics and Strategy*, a bimonthly journal. It's website includes reports and analyses such as "Unease Grows over Syria's Chemical Weapons," and "Making Sense of Syria."

Middle East Policy Council

1730 M St. NW, Ste. 512, Washington, DC 20036-4505
(202) 296-6767 • fax: (202) 296-5791
e-mail: info@mepc.org
website: www.mepc.org

The Middle East Policy Council was founded in 1981 to expand public discussion and understanding of issues affecting U.S. policy in the Middle East. The council is a nonprofit educational organization that operates nationwide. It publishes the quarterly *Middle East Policy Journal* and offers workshops for secondary-level educators on how to teach students about the Arab world and Islam.

Middle East Research and Information Project (MERIP)

1500 Massachusetts Ave. NW, Washington, DC 20005

(202) 223-3677 • fax: (202) 223-3604
website: www.merip.org

MERIP is a nonprofit, nongovernmental organization with no links to any religious, educational, or political organizations in the United States or elsewhere. MERIP feels that understanding of the Middle East in the United States and Europe is limited and plagued by stereotypes and misconceptions. The project strives to end these limitations by addressing a broad range of social, political, and cultural issues and by soliciting writings and views from authors from the Middle East who are not often read in the West. Its newsletter, *Middle East Report*, is published four times a year, and MERIP offers an extensive list of other Middle Eastern Internet resources. Articles available on its website include "Syria and Lebanon: A Brotherhood Transformed," and "Change and Status in Syria."

US Department of State

Bureau of Near Eastern Affairs, Washington, DC   20520
(202) 647-4000
website: www.state.gov/p/nea/

The Bureau of Near Eastern Affairs deals with US foreign policy and relations with the countries in the Middle East and North Africa. Its website offers country information as well as news briefings, press statements, and transcripts of congressional testimony related to the Middle East.

Washington Institute for Near East Policy

1828 L St. NW, Ste. 1050, Washington, DC   20036
(202) 452-0650 • fax: (202) 223-5364
e-mail: info@washingtoninstitute.org
website: www.washingtoninstitute.org

The institute is an independent organization that produces research and analysis on the Middle East and on US policy in the region. It publishes numerous position papers and reports on Arab and Israeli politics and social developments. It also publishes position papers on Middle Eastern military issues and US policy, including "Chemical Reaction: How the United States Should Deal with Assad."

Bibliography of Books

Fouad Ajami   *The Syrian Rebellion*. Stanford, CA: Hoover Institution Press, 2012.

Brooke Allen   *The Other Side of the Mirror: An American Travels Through Syria*. Philadelphia: Paul Dry Books, 2011.

Ross Burns   *Damascus: A History*. New York: Routledge, 2007.

Anthony H. Cordesman, Aram Nerguizian, and Inout C. Popescu   *Israel and Syria: The Military Balance and Prospects of War*. Westport, CT: Praeger, 2009.

Nikolaos van Dam   *The Struggle for Power in Syria: Politics and Society Under Asad and the Ba'th Party*. Revised and updated edition. New York: Tauris, 2011.

Simon Dunstan   *The Six Day War 1967: Jordan and Syria*. Oxford: Osprey, 2009.

James L. Gelvin   *The Arab Uprisings: What Everyone Needs to Know*. New York: Oxford University Press, 2012.

Philip K. Hitti   *History of Syria, Including Lebanon and Palestine*. Vol. 1. Piscataway, NJ: Gorgias, 2002.

David W. Lesch   *The Fall of the House of Assad*. New Haven, CT: Yale University Press, 2012.

David W. Lesch — *The New Lion of Damascus: Bashar al-Assad and Modern Syria.* New Haven, CT: Yale University Press, 2005.

Flynt Leverett — *Inheriting Syria: Bashar's Trial by Fire.* Washington, DC: Brookings, 2005.

Marc Lynch — *The Arab Uprising: The Unfinished Revolutions of the New Middle East.* New York: PublicAffairs, 2013.

Moshe Ma'oz, Joseph Ginat, Onn Winckler, eds. — *Modern Syria: From Ottoman Rule to Pivotal Role in the Middle East.* East Sussex, UK: Sussex Academic, 1999.

Andrew McCarthy — *Spring Fever: The Illusion of Islamic Democracy.* New York: Encounter Books, 2013.

Lin Noueihed and Alex Warren — *The Battle for the Arab Spring: Revolution, Counter-Revolution and the Making of a New Era.* New Haven, CT: Yale University Press, 2012.

Volker Perthes — *Syria Under Bashar al-Asad: Modernisation and the Limits of Change.* New York: Routledge, 2004.

Thomas Pierret — *Religion and State in Syria: The Sunni Ulama from Coup to Revolution.* New York: Cambridge University Press, 2013.

Robert G. Rabil — *Syria, The United States, and the War on Terror in the Middle East.* Westport, CT: Praeger, 2006.

Barry Rubin — *The Truth About Syria.* New York: Palgrave Macmillan, 2008.

Stephen Starr — *Revolt in Syria: Eye-Witness to the Uprising.* New York: Columbia University Press, 2012.

Andrew Tabler — *In the Lion's Den: An Eyewitness Account of Washington's Battle with Syria.* Chicago: Chicago Review Press, 2011.

Nasser Weddady and Sohrab Ahmari, eds. — *Arab Spring Dreams: The Next Generation Speaks Out for Freedom and Justice from North Africa to Iran.* New York: Palgrave Macmillan, 2012.

Carsten Wieland — *Syria—A Decade of Lost Chances: Repression and Revolution from Damascus Spring to Arab Spring.* Seattle: Cune, 2012.

Samar Yazbek — *A Woman in the Crossfire: Diaries of the Syrian Revolution.* Translated by Max Weiss. London: Haus, 2012.

Radwan Ziadeh — *Power and Policy in Syria: Intelligence Services, Foreign Relations and Democracy in the Modern Middle East.* New York: Tauris, 2011.

Index

S

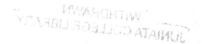